MW00682568

Stars in Our Hearts
Musings

Suzanne Hilary

EDITOR

World Poetry Movement

Utah

Stars in Our Hearts: Musings

Library of Congress
Cataloging in Publication Data

ISBN 978-1-60880-140-4

Printed and manufactured in the United States of America by

World Poetry Movement
Utah

Foreword

I would like to take this opportunity to welcome all of our newly-published poets to the World Poetry Movement. By sharing your work with a larger audience, you have joined us in our pursuit to keep the art of poetry alive and thriving today. At WPM, we work with great purpose and genuinely believe anyone can achieve poetic success with the right amount of determination. Walt Whitman once said, "To have great poets, there must be great audiences," and our goal is to continue feeding and building today's poetry community. Right now, our nation is full of both budding and seasoned artists whose poetry has received national recognition, which also means that writers must also be readers in order for such recognition to be possible. By showcasing the work of aspiring writers and putting it out there for all to see, we hope to keep more readers and writers of all levels engaged to this artform. Any accomplished writer will agree that to become a better writer it is essential to also be an audience by reading the works of others just as often as one writes. To fellow aspiring poets, each individual poem in this collection shares a unique source of inspiration, offers a new idea or perspective, and/or displays a creative way to express sentiment and emotion. We hope you find just as much pleasure in reading the verse throughout as you do in composing your own. In the meantime, keep writing, keep sharing, and keep those dreams close to your heart!

Suzanne Hilary
Editor

.

Combat Boots

My old friends, scuffed and battered,
You greet me, tongues extended,
Ready for another patrol, another
Perhaps perdition.

We've come far, so far,
Muck-smeared, wearing
Blood of foes and yes, of friends
In death conjoined.

Walking point, guts locked, awaiting the
Snap of an unseen wire,
Betty's bounce, a blast
Too fast to hear.

Yet we survived, came home to
Sere, savage shores,
Where we were cursed, reviled,
Rejected, cast aside.

Consigned to junk piles,
Tongues extended, asking only
For drops of kindness,
From wells of love gone dry.

Edward Weiss

Unbelievable

You're unbelievable,
I'm out of my mind,
Head over heals for you
And I want you to know
That I'd do anything just to be in your world.
And I'd do anything just to be your girl.

You're so amazing,
It's hard to figure you out.
That's why I'm gazin',
wondering what you're all about.

Mackenzie Neely

You and I

I wish I wish,
Oh how I wish,
Your tender lips,
Would grant a kiss,
I love you so,
But you cannot see,
That you and I,
Are meant to be.

Mackenzie Powell

Without Friends

Without friends there would be no flowers blooming
Without friends the sun wouldn't gleam and glow
There would be no ocean waves
Or stars above us
But most importantly
Without friends there wouldn't be people
who accept us for who we are.

Kristina Tobler

Metalurgy

The Word calls me the silver, My Lord, he builds the fire
This world is like a caldron, changing all my heart's desire
Forging tests the haughty spirit, then reminds me of my goal
Lets me simmer 'til I hear it…purify my molten soul..
Spinning, rolling, boiling metal, as my mind wants to explode
Imperfections, rising, settle…dross is lifted from its hold
Testing to refine my strength, As my faith grows higher, higher
Take me to my finest length, only God can calm the fire
My Lord, the Metalurgist, this body's like a lump of coal
tempered, soothing love he give turning silver into gold
When I peer into the silver, no remembrance do I see
Just God's image in the mirror, where this tempest used to be.

Wanda Beardslee

Everything's Seasonal

A fresh new flower at the peek of my season.
Plenty of rain; to complain there's no reason.
It's sunny and bright, I'm such a beautiful sight.
I'll bloom here all summer—who knows, maybe longer?
There are no people, no wheels, no mongrels.
I think I'll remain here forevermore,
since all the bugs, they adore.
My radiant colors leap out at their eyes,
even prettier to the dirty old flies.
It seems chilly; leaves fall all around;
they look much bigger once on the ground.
But the grass isn't green!
No flies to be seen as well as the weeds.
My colors are faded, I feel so degraded.
There is a large blanket which looks like thick dew.
No bug here to say, "Never have I seen such one as you."
I'm covered and cold, I almost feel old.
I no longer feel superior; remarkably inferior
.I had a good year, until now I knew no such fear.
I had never been picked, never been kicked.
I was great 'til the end—no more to be said.
I was better than all, but it's well past fall.
It seems I'm no better than any seasonal flower.
I never had much power … I guess I'm just a seasonal flower.

Josie Williams

Mr. President Obama, I Want . . .

Mankind to be kinder to man
the world to echo the belief *yes we can*
children to live without fear
equality to be truly equal
life to be valued higher than gold

The tally of one's true legacy
to be measured by their mercy
law to always speak the truth
the plague of racism to be vanquished
for earth's bounty to feed the hungry

The games we play called war
to be declared forever lost
the blindness of all hate
to be granted sight and tolerance
the cries of the weak and abused
to be answered by the strong

Our rain forests to be cherished
whales to roam free within pristine seas
the words spoken *never again*
to never again be needed to be said
every man to be a brother of mine
each child to be my child

Within my lifetime

Michael Poyntz

Thank You, Heath

For all of my life I was not in view.
I was frightened, scared to be me.
Hidden away I stayed cloaked in fear
waiting for....
In awe I saw it, full of love and hope.
All leaves shimmering in blue.
Heath, I became me because of you.
You gave me light.
Your laughter makes me happy.
Your smile warms my heart.
Your fearlessness gives me courage.
Your kindness gives me hope.
You made me believe in everything.
Your death gave me appreciation.
Even through great grief and deep pain,
I learned that you are beautiful
because you do not know that you are.
The very most important thing you gave me, Heath,
was the courage to learn that I could indeed dance in the rain.
Thank You, Heath.

Melissa Zilkie

Bliss Goes Beyond Ignorance

Fingerprints on the window
From days of longing for freedom

All I hear is the sound of my own heart
All I know is that I don't know anything

Another second passes where I should fall apart.

Derek Friesen

Cupid's Arrow

I don't know why
you make me cry
or why I still love you
after you do
But for some reason,
Cupid's arrow is deeply
embedded in my skin.
And when I think about you
all my thoughts wear thin.
The more I try to rip it out,
the deeper it goes in.
Looks like Cupid's arrow
will forever be
within me...

Lexi Sandell

Written All Over My Body

Foggy and unclean,
all I want to do is scream.
For no reason, with no rhyme,
you left me here to die.

The persistence of memory haunts me,
like a thief it steals my sleep
and I can't remember what it's like to be happy,
the way we used to be.

When you slipped you're hand into mine,
you could read the smile dancing on my lips,
and our passionate whispers were like a symphony,
when all you needed was me.

The painful memories give birth to a feeling of loss,
a hole in my chest; a missing heart that is lost,
a gut-wrenching sadness that leaves me gasping.

No longer thirsting for sleep,
but for us together.
You carved my heart in two,
and I stayed up, cursing you.

I pull my hands through my hair over and over,
hoping this isn't really our closure.
Black tears run down from my eyes,
staining the bed in which I lie.

Now the pain is written on my body—
not through cuts and scrapes,
From ink—my own therapy.

Fake tattoos, black and blue
the ink decorates my body,
and easy way to change me
and still remember you.

Whether it's hidden with clothes or on display,
all these symbols point to you,
a way to remember us two.

The elaborate designs
remind me of the time when you were mine
Say it's a way to get over you,
But only I know the truth:

I keep writing these every day to remind me
how vulnerable I was, but how I still felt safe,
to remind me of how I felt when I saw your face.
This is me keeping our memories alive,
written all over my body.

Amber Powers

Journey of My Soul

The moon's glow embraced my body,
   Enraptured by a presence that felt most Godly.
I closed my eyes and felt a sense of peace,
   I was so light, I joined the stars with ease.
A shooting star carried me into the depths of the sky,
   I could feel my soul on this journey high.
I had no pain, I had no fears,
   I wept with joy, yet, I had no tears.
Comets whooshed by at tremendous speeds,
   I followed bright auras to see where they'd lead.
A universe of beauty hidden in the darkness
   Life so grand, waiting for something greater to embark in.
I gasped at the serenity and grandeur of it all.
   Yet, I had no breath when I answered its call.
I was within the breath and soul of life,
   Fearing not death for I journey open-eyed.
I am not dead but most certainly alive,
   I've touched upon God within the abyss of the sky.
It is there I found life's first perfect breath.
   Meditation for the soul within its depth.

Diana Vela

Dreams

Dreams are free spirits.
Dreams are glee on a bad day.
A bad dream can scare you.
A sad dream might make you cry.
Dreams are all around you,
Floating, prancing, and soaring really high.
At night the dreams come out.
Don't worry dreams don't bite or fight.
Dreams are free spirits they cannot be closed in.
A closed-in dream will get angry and become a bad dream.

Marc Vermette

Real Beauty

The sun rises up,
I see beauty,
hues of orange, red, and pink,
meanwhile, we sink down,
I see pain,
shades of blue, black, and gray,
but isn't that life?

Sabrina Guzman

I Cannot Eat My Soup

I cannot eat my soup
Because there a fly has landed
I yelled for him to leave
Yet he only remained candid
I cannot eat my soup
Because in it the fly did swim
So I took my spoon and around the bowl
I started to chase him
I cannot eat my soup
Because the chase made it slosh
When I tried to flick him out
Now everything needs a wash
I cannot eat my soup
Because when the fly finally flew
I looked down to my bowl
To see my soup was gone too

Sarai Smith

No One's Reflection

Sometimes you'll feel content,
Other times it'll feel like you don't know,
Who you are at all.
Only you can choose who you want to be,
But you should be no one but yourself.
Like a snowflake,
Not one person is alike,
But even you seem to stand out,
In the uniquest of crowds,
I know you're different,
Perfect isn't a large enough word.
I don't think I'll ever meet anyone,
Quite as special as you.
You seem to believe the taunts in the mirror,
Confused by the eyes staring back.
You seem to push away the truth,
Of the guy in the mirror. . .
To truly see who he really is.
Don't read yourself by chapter,
But page by page.
Push away the lies,
See the truth in who you are. . .
Don't be too quick to judge yourself on mistakes,
Judge by accomplishments and try till you succeed.
Don't dwell on the past,
You're in the present.
Count the times you have helped someone,
You may have even saved a life just by smiling,
Not even knowing you kept a heart beating.
Throw away the key to the lock,
That is the truth on your side of the mirror,
Don't ever read a reflection,
For it isn't the original on the other side of the mirror . . .
"To be yourself in a world that is constantly trying
to change you, is the greatest accomplishment."

Dre Burke

Cyber Love

Though many miles separate us
I still see your lovely smile
Feel the softness of your touch
The passion in our kisses

I feel a strong attraction
The closing of the miles
Our keyboards are our voices
Our hearts our connections

Feel the love we send
On wings of Caber doves
Our hopes, our dreams
Our needs, our wants

They make deliveries
Of touches, caresses, love
Never to my recollection
Has love been so vivid?

Mind to mind, heart to heart
That's where it starts
Then goes on, now and forever

Charles White

Switch

Your faith saves your life.
Your faith heals your pain

Faith and doubts are
like position On and position Off

Even though an accomplished doctor touches your body
Even though a mysterious shaman performs ritual
Even though a full-of-Spirit pastor prays on your head

If your faith,
If your switch is still off

Your incurable disease cannot be broken up

In spite of tremendous power from a huge nuclear plant,
even a little bulb cannot let it shine, if your switch is still off

Seongchoon Pak

Basketball and Life

Basketball is just a game,
but with passion and love
it is so much more.

It is just a game until you throw your body
to the ground for a loose ball
then you add hustle
and now its competition.
You play every day and now it's a lifestyle.
If you don't work on the court
you will never work hard in life.
Without hard work nothing is worth doing
if it's not to your full potential.

Kristian Teschner

My Life

My life relies on you
Don't deny the only truth
I miss you when the Rain
Falls down
I miss you when the Sun
Is shining
I love you more than rain and sun
And even still when there is none

Estelle King

Red, White and Blue

To my dear Red, White and Blue
Every day I think of you.
Every privilege and every right
Every being who stood up to fight.
Every freedom
We proudly use.
Freedom to love
And freedom to choose,
Freedom to read
And freedom to muse.
Freedom to care
And freedom to bear.
With our many freedoms and rights,
Who wouldn't, who couldn't
Stand up to fight.

Jessica Shanken

My Love Story

We walk among the shadows
We hide in despair
Where glutton in our depression
And angered of ourselves
Gratuitous banter I hear one day
A grudging pull felt my heart away
A hapless life I lived one day
Where love was gloomy
Where pain was gusto,
to the hallowed days
As I sit here pondering
About life and its ways
I look at you
But love is in the way
So I banish in the dark
Fearing you one day will hear me say
That love is an object
There's nothing else I can say
As I watch the people in my room
Heretic, hypocrites saying I am wrong
To put my hands together
And pray the pain away
Love is not visible
Nothing to hold
Nothing to feel
It's just an object
A transvestite feeling
A gullible ploy
To happiness sham
Nothing is tangible
We live in a desensitized society
Where people die in self-torment

Gabriel Ambros

Only One Sacrifice—a Villanelle

He came to save, He came to die—
His Sacrifice encompassed all
beneath the shadows of the sky.

Men mock and jeer with jaundiced eye—
their bitter hearts do not recall
He came to save, He came to die.

"Behold Thy Son." Who will reply?
His blood, as drops of payment fall,
beneath the shadows of the sky.

The Magdalen is standing nigh—
His Mother gazes, strong and small.
He came to save, He came to die.

In pain he hangs— the wind keens by,
they offer vinegar and gall
beneath the shadows of the sky.

At last it comes! He gives a cry!
His blood is spent—He's given all.
He came to save, He came to die,
beneath the shadows of the sky.

Katrina DeLallo

Restoration

I was once restored and cured from the light
I refused to see as my eyes remained closed,
but thru purpose and change I saw a replenished force
and that the sight I had once before was the motive to remain on the
right side instead of steering left into a lane of destruction,
but in that lane I noticed I had another way of transporting my life
right
again

Restoration mixed with confidence,
faith, wisdom and choice to change in moderation
from a young boy to a young man to one day become a man "the man"
that was already destined in a line of loving for love
and leaving hate behind me for those who live a path
of being unreal with themselves which in a way shows the truth
within their eyes aside from their actions falsified
by fighting the true person who lies within

Growing and maturing but being more confident
in knowing as I pray for what we need as people
instead of what we want, but in that journey
we must force our line of sight on the path ahead
for sacrifices will be made for myself but for others as well
in the process of this restoration in life and love
because without them both I know I wouldn't be the man you see
before you today being a new man spiritually tomorrow

Restoration

Ryan Brown

When Someone Dies

When someone you love passes away
you feel broken

in every way.
One day you look back

but you really don't want to look back.

You have memories in your head

that you never want to let go of.

But when that someone passes away
you're lost inside

and you just want to cry.

Samantha Stewart

When You Said to Move On

you said you will move on and to do the same
how you want me to do that when i love you
i really don't know what to do
is it for you just a game

when you told me that i wasn't myself anymore
i wanted to stay with you more
it was you that had decided to break up
i guess i run out of luck

the breaking up had hit me really hard
now i feel you really far
i can barely sleep now
some days i just want to cry out loud

i miss you and think a lot about you
every day I think about what I should do
I just want you back around
without you I feel so down

Melanie Beaulieu

The Broken Girl

Think about it, dream about it, every day she wants it
But the world is so against her, and now she thinks she's lost it.
So she buries her dreams and hide her tears,
And now all she has left is fears.

Who is this girl who used to fly so high?
For she's lost her bright, she's lost her fight,
Still wondering who will be there to help her ignite
And clear her cloudy, stormy sky?

There she is: her own worst enemy, a liar, a killer
Fooling herself in fear of the pain,
The smile on her face keeping the questions away
And drowning her beautiful hope because she can't sustain.

Afraid of her reflection, because she'll see every fault
Her thoughts acting as her own assault.
She strives for perfection, yet always falls short
With tear-filled eyes the truth she can't help but distort.

She waits for salvation, for she knows there's a cure
To help her forget what her mind made her endure.
Love is the riddle, yet love is the answer (is it only a trick?)
Share the love or love herself, wishing one day it will all just click.

Andrea Papari

Truthiness in Literacy

Always resistant, ever stubborn to mother's wishes
Let me be up in the trees
Not buried below in the resulting product of them
Laborious, snail-paced, required
Give me a moving image, thank you very much
Leave the stagnant, stationary syllables to the squares
If you need me, nerds
I will be among the trees

Joel Ewing

In the Light of Memory

Let her soul drift away in peace, harmony.
Upon a breath, inhaled, exhaled.
Within the vessel, lit for all to see.

A great love, life lost to a tragic end.
Surrounded by all she'll forever love.
A whisper carries out the light to mend,

Not the cry, nor the tear, but the memory.
Only to be long held, like a newborn.
The love always there in her legacy.

Brock Koch

By the Bay

Trees I have seen
On this hot summer's day.
I focus on the leaves between
and the ripples on the bay.

The noises are sharp as a harp
played by the beloved heart.
Oh, how beautiful the day
is being played by the bay.

Clint Bowman

A Rose

A rose has thorns without those thorns a rose is just another flower, the thorns make her original without equal, there is no other who can take her place.

Her beauty goes further then the others because she comes in more than one color like the woman of today, who are all different colors like the beautiful rose.

Which makes us all unique.

The other flowers are just the followers who try to be the rose, so which one do you want to be?

Tiana Gumpert

An End to Pride

A grand masquerade ball.
The hidden faces grinning.
The tower of lies is oh so tall.
They all appear to be laughing.

I sit at my throne,
watching them all prance.
All but one is a drone.
The music plays, and they all begin to dance.

I rise to my feet,
And walk into the fray.
My sword is drawn, I match the beat.
As they fall, they begin to pray.

The fury subsides, it is done.
All that remains is one.

Dalton Kraus

Walking in the Rain

all eyes on him
as the service begins
sorrow and grief
as we were all struck with misbelief
a man I knew
so young and so strong
felt so alone in this world
where he felt he didn't belong
I know this feeling as most do
you lose someone close
and your heart fades to blue
at midnight that night
he took his own life
the pain from suicide
cuts like a knife
as the time has gone on
I will always feel that pain
but I will always remember
you with your umbrella
walking in the rain

Jacquelyn Barnlund

To My Soul Mate

I don't know who you are
or if I have the merits
to pursue my desire
to finally find you.

A burning sensation
knowing you're out there
searching for me
but I wasn't there.

Long time had passed
and you did not find me
because I was lost
nowhere to find me.

I talked to the Lord
and asked for the wisdom
just part the Red sea
and she will be there.

You need to work hard
beyond recognition.
Life is all in your heart
and also your hands.

You need to be patient
like never before
you need to bring light
because that is the purpose.

Hector Muniz

The Bitter Truth

We think we know who we are, but we don't.
We believe we know right from wrong, but do we really?
We pretend not to hear them, but the scars are just as deep.
And one day we won't be able to heal them.
We act as if we don't care, but we can't fool ourselves.
We listen to the lies that we are loved, but the message doesn't sink in.
We lie to protect ourselves, but is it worth it?
Only the end will tell.
We tell them we follow our heart,
but we can only hide the truth for so long.
We cover up the scars, but weakness finds a way through.
We hide behind our masks, but they'll dissolve sooner or later.
Sometimes it's too late.
We live the lies,
We hide the truth.
We know nothing,
We say we do.
We think we know who we are, but we don't.
And that's the truth.

Kayla Britton

You Try and Want

You try so hard,
Try too much
You can't fix this mess of me,
Nor this twisted mind I have
Can't stop what I do—
What I have done
You try, but you don't succeed
You want me to live
To be happy—
Happy and smile
But I can't
Too many haunting memories
So very many bad thoughts
Nightmares galore
Every single night
You try so hard,
Want so much
But you just can't succeed—
Not in fixing me,
Nor in my happiness.

Jennie Bird

Distant

It's a vast nothingness,
An eternity of fate.
My world is crumbling,
Nothing to take its place.

The distance between us is deafening.
I cannot hear you shout.
You cannot see me move.
We are a million miles away.

Distant.

Ashley Philipp

I Love You

Staring at an empty room
Wondering what I did to make you leave
You're gone, you vanished
and with that you took my heart
You have to understand I'm not perfect
No one is, but we were a perfect couple
I can't proclaim this feeling
Every song I hear reminds me of you
Why is my breath gone?
Why do I feel so empty?
I need you, come back
I love you.

Julie Ramos

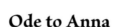

Ode to Anna

You loved me
like a mother,
with your eyes
blue as the sky
staring back at me
through the frame
of the picture.
I realize how
much I miss
you but I
know you're
always in my
heart and I
wonder if
I'll ever see
you again . . .
I wish I could.
I love you
like a mother
with my eyes
stone cold blue
staring back at you
as you wonder if
you will hear
from me again.
And I answer in
my thoughts and
say "when my
time comes I'll
see and hear you
again."

Mickayla Van Strydonk

Sailor, Dream

Soul; A honeyed tidal without ebb, and when I put my lips to her I get a taste. Her beauteous bones, arresting, on my pallet, catching my eye more quickly than I my breath. And as she rises, she arches. She will come, zealous: a grace amidst ease, to me.

Bonnie Hickman

An Honest Poem

Just an honest poem 'bout a pretty girl
And one in which I'm sure you can relate
For as you know my head's in a twirl
Also as you know love does complicate
Time slows down as my eyes fall upon her
Nerves fail, my hand quivers, I drop my cup
We talk; she understands how I want her
But as it's just a dream I must wake up
Life is a short trip, too short without her
Her beauty rips my heart with searing chains
Whatever I weather I will need her
I will be bound forever in her chains
I pray to Aphrodite; let it be
Falling to my knees I pray let it be!

Esiban Parent

Guardian Angel

My wings beat in rhythm with the thundering night,
My way is lit when lightning crackles bright.
The thunder overpowers the needy world,
Cries are drowned out and lies are unfurled.
With a flash of lightning my heart skips a beat,
I fall fast from the sky feeling an angry heat.
A beast awaits me, it walks the broken streets,
The thunder buries my voice and hides my tear stained cheeks.
The beast ripped away my wings, I have no place to go,
I hear its angry growl and I wait for its final blow.
I close my eyes tight and brace for the pain,
But instead comes the gentle touch of the kissing rain.
A protecting hand takes mine and helps me to my feet,
It moves the stray hair from my eyes and the lost tears from my cheeks.
I've fallen in love and I know we'll never part,
He's my guardian angel and he holds my beating heart.

Ashley Brewer

Life

when you close your eyes do you see anything?
when does life get better any?
do we need dreams to see the things that are clear enough to see?
do we really need everything we need?
when does want become need?
the stars are bright but not like the light you see when you're on the
edge of your destiny,
when you slowly fade into the night and your entire life flashes by
and you can only think and wonder why
why is your life ending so early?
you get to live and then you die
why is life unfair in the middle?
life sucks and that's a fact we can't change it but only hope for the best
we can love and we can cry
and even when they ask us why
no matter what the sky is blue
so just keep on pushing through
when you think it's all over, it's never over until you take your life
but for now you've got to choose,
make your life keep on moving
and always ask yourself—
what's going to happen next?

Jordann Martinez

Eternity Labyrinth

In the quiet serene of the dark,
A gentle wind blows softly.
And through the vine-covered passages,
There is no light to guide me.

Many a time I've passed a route barricaded with lianas,
Thorns protruding everywhere, making it hard to pass.
Sadly, shimmers of light peek through the gaps,
But I couldn't get through the vines to the light.

My heart aches for the light, but I blindly trudge on,
My bare feet freeze on the cold hard ground,
Caressed by the breeze I am, but never by the light.
As I pass another thorn blocked track, I stop and stare.

Light glimmers through the gaps once more, drawing me in.
I narrow my eyes at the barrier, each thorn blood-tipped:
others tried to pass.
I know others have died trying, but I won't be one of them.
I wish to be free of the dark; I wish to be in the light.

I break through the wall, but not without wounds.
Blood soaks my hair giving it a reddish sheen,
The passage on this end is filled with light,
And I know, as I walk the Eternity Labyrinth in the light, I am free.

Heather Stephens

Nightmare

your lies fuel this fire
my freedom is what i desire
my words will lift me higher
you gotta let me go
so i can fly
trying to let my spirit soar high
i will never have an impact is what i fear
my date with destiny is near
my mind is filled with failed tries
pulled down by this world's lies
all i hear is the angels' cries
and yet i try
i can't run so i crawl
i try to stand but crumble and fall
how can i stand tall
when my back is broken
so many words left unspoken
i open my eyes but can't see
i look up and ask God why me
just let this tormented soul be
I've given up so now i hide
torn and terrified inside
i think back on the times I've lied
the times I've cried
but now all i can think about is being alone
lost to remain in the unknown
like a planted seed I've grown
"even though I walk through the valley of the shadow of death,
I will fear no evil,"
But I do fear
My imminent death is near
I lay on the grass down my face rolls a tear
So I turn to the sky think about what i should say

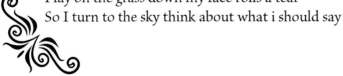

I can't so I begin to pray
Asking God to forgive what I've done
Away goes the sun
I try to run
As I gravitate to a gun
I put it to my head
I squeeze the ground turns red
I begin to scream
I wake and realize this was all a dream

Edward Tritsch

Always Remember

We each own a part of the Master Key
From the day we met and I laid my eyes upon you
It was very clear to see
One day you would be a part of me
We said our vows
And shortly after that a family we had come to be
Laughter, joy, pain and sorrow
We always looked forward to tomorrow
Though our circumstances have changed
Please try and understand
This was part of our Lord's master plan
So take a deep breath and know this is true
Because I will always and forever love you

Shelly Coker

Something

I walked through
The silent roar of the unknown
Where life was few
And all else was gone
The fiery cold
Was all around
The land was old
There was no sound
My mind wonders
Though clear as mud
The sky thunders
My footsteps thud
I ran fast
Though I found nothing
In the past
I lost something.

Layla Henson

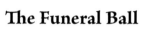

The Funeral Ball

Ladies and demons, now come one, come all.
You're all invited to this funeral ball,
A death masquerade of all things divine.
I seek nothing more than a corpse to make mine.

So take off your skin and come right on in.
The only thing present here is deep, dark sin.
The music is heavy, sharp as a knife,
Representing our newfound underground life.

It's amazing, it's obscene,
Grotesque, and everything in between.
Line up, right here, and wait your turn.
You'll get your chance to stand and to burn.

The music quickens, a frightening pace,
Slamming through your body, echoing in space.
The spirits, they spin, they whirl, they fly,
Who knows? Maybe you'll be the next to die.

Then you'll be mine, my corpse forever.
Ha! You, released from me? But never!
I'll keep you here, to have and to hold.
Your body is mine, it's already been sold.

Your protests mean nothing, it's already too late.
There's nothing you can do to escape your fate.
The music, still faster, will plague your mind.
Ensuing insanity is all you'll find.

When death takes over, my corpse you'll be
I'll keep you forever, you won't be free.
Come dance with me, my very dear soul,
Death's dance is the last thing you'll ever behold.

I'll tear you to pieces, rip you to shreds.
None of this will matter once you are dead.
Now come, my darling, come to me.
Stuck here forever, my corpse you will be.

Iggy Turner

Peeping Pirates

The virtue of innocence provides a gallivanting mind
The mermaids, the ships, the pirates combined
As the waves of the sea come to their crest
I see Blackbeard's crew put to the test
The glitter of the ocean makes me believe
Their treasure is true, I say, diamonds, rubies, gold to retrieve
Pelicans become parrots, sailboats to ships
The salt in the air becomes rum on a pirate's lips
Blackbeard shouts for the sails, "crank, crank, crank"
As fear fills my bones when the pier becomes the plank
Shiny fish swimming at my feet beneath
Become giant sharks with glistening teeth
I close my eyes to the peeping pirates of the sea
Wanting, wishing, praying, it was all just a dream to me

Kayla Martin

Lifeless Hope

She sat there...
Hoping and praying
that maybe someday
she would have
the strength
to carry on
and live her life
without
the constant interruption
of life itself...
The way depression
has permanently
altered her life
without any hope
and prayers left
for her
to rely on.

Morgan Puddy

Control

She locks the door.
Alone in her room, she can't hold back.
She cries the tears she didn't want to shed.
She screams and raves, frustrated.
She needs to control at least one thing in her life.
She needs an outlet for the emotions she refuses to express.
For when she did express, she was ordered to repress them.
She grabs the knife.
She wants to take her own life.
She's sick of the yelling, sick of the fighting.
She's fighting in an endless war.
Nobody really wins.
She's sick of the pain.
She turns emotional pain and scars into physical ones
on her wrists and arms.
She sighs in content as the cool steel breaks the dam of soft flesh
and releases the crimson river her pain flows within,
letting both stream away in streaks of red.
She won't do it tonight.
Not when she finally has control.
She can hold on one more time.
She finally has a way to control her pain,
and she won't let them stop her.

Ericka Healy

The Art of Beauty

As I admire the silhouette of your beautiful frame
I stand and think, what a masterpiece what is her name
As your beauty hangs upon the wall, that creates my thoughts
My mind wanders and can't be caught
I was once told, beauty is in the eye of the beholder
That means when God thought of beauty He became your Creator
As you sway to the rhythm of my beating heart
Our souls intertwine like they grew together and never apart
The world around me diminished and you are all I see
I would surrender to your love, gloriously
The mind of a man that has been overtaken by love
Creates his own world that cherishes His love
Fake or fiction this is my reality,
How can I part from my definition of beauty

Antoine Davis

At twenty-three I am enlisted in the United States Navy, and my inspiration for poetry comes from the thought of inspiring those who need inspiration for them to move forward and also for those who need to feel warmth within their heart.

Off and Away But Still Here

You're gone now
And while I shall never see you again
I know you will always be here
Always by my side
Though I didn't know you long
I know enough to never forget
Every time we spoke I will remember
Every time I saw you, I will remember
Though your soul is gone
Taken by the injustice of the world
I have the memories
And knowing you will go to paradise
Will comfort me
And the burning desire to see you avenged
You're off and away
To a place I can't follow yet
And yet when I close my eyes
You're still here with me

Cassidy Woody

Words of the Quiet One

They tried to change me, but they failed.
They tried to hurt me when I was frail.
Others thirsted for my tears, but I showed them no fear.
I stay strong with my mind where my heart is, and go where people forbid.
Yes they talk, and yes they speak.
But someday they will walk the earth knowing I am not meek.
I keep my head up high with determination struck in my eyes.
Back straight and a smile on my face,
I don't need anyone to be my brace.
I hear the dos and don'ts, but listen to any of them I won't.
I go where destiny takes me, and destroy where people try to make me.
I lead my future and forget my past.
But every moment I have left, I shall make it last.

Alejandra Cano

I am a fourteen-year-old incoming freshman. My passions are creative writing and basketball, along with drawing. I believe I inherited my talents from my grandmother who was crafty and artistic, and my father who is a Grammy Award-winning artist. Poetry has always been the most freeing way to express how I feel inside. Whether I am feeling happy or sad, poetry has always been there to get me through the tough times. This poem was inspired by the people who tried to make me something I wasn't. But no matter what happened, I always had to remember who I really was. Thanks to this poem, I have found the strength to show them who I really am.

My Suicide Letter

When I die I wish for everyone to feel the same pain as I have in my life. I don't want to owe anything to anyone for I am the one everyone has despised, and yes these are my last words in the event of my demise. As I longed for my purpose, I abandoned my soul and began a never-ending circuit. It consisted of pain, depression, and certainly never happiness. Pleasure never existed in me, neither has humanity. There is no going back now, my heart has sunk deeply in the depths of solitude, causing my spirit to be less profound, and yes my purpose has never been found. Sometimes I'd get caught up in the pressure of it all and cry until I'd be lost, but I can crawl until I can walk again, but then again my ambition to thrive is just not as tall. I lost it through my ways of trying to find a trace of happiness, but if you just listen to this, you'd wish to save me, but of course this life wasn't made for me. I walk without feeling, just thinking about it is rather chilling. I want to at least taste something, feed my soul, be reborn and come back as something rather than nothing. It's too late to save me, but it can't be goodbye for now. My spirit now feels profound, and yes my purpose has now been found. This has been God's plan for me as Heaven forever holds my crown. There comes a time when the sun will bring together the east side and west, causing them to collide and til then I will remain mutual 'cause the blood from a soldier's wounds are the teardrops God cries. Do not cut life short for this is God's prize. We do not want to come off weak as we talk of our demise. Just until then life gets better and you begin to think there isn't a reason for a suicide letter.

Kylie Whittaker

This Is Where I'm From

I am from tire swings, slip-n-slides, and climbing trees
Running around barefoot and rolling down hills

I am from Nancy Drew and Dy-No-Mite
Pop Rocks and football

I am from Queen and the Partridge Family
Coca-Cola and old records

I am from a small town with a small family
I am from Winne the Pooh and Blue's Clues

I am from an old carboard box,
Filled to the top of forgotten faces and places.

Abigail Walsh

We Are One

My heart beats for every moment of our armored love.
My head spins rapidly with confusing but engaging thoughts of how it
all came to be.
I ponder and realize our outer selves are not who we are in reality.
I am undoubtedly humble, I am a mere silhouette of insecurity and grief.
You are enraged and heartbroken but you disguise it with your
empathic love for me.
We know each other from our distressing youths.
We breathe the same everlasting air.
We walk on the same rocky pavement that brings us both back to
yesteryears.
Our families intrude on our affairs because they can't grasp our
gratifying wonder.
We both just brush their words away as if they fell on deaf ears.
We hold each other tight, gluttonously until we both fall into a
meditative sleep.
I dream of you as you dream of me, our dreams collide and our minds
spark with emotions that are unseen to the loveless eye.
We both know our love is strong and compelling—you have the power
to kill me my love.
I know you hold my heart in your hand when I simply just turn a blind
eye when you speak.
I know you are ripping at the seems of your heart every time I utter
crucifying words I never mean to speak.
You know I am not one for small talk at parties so you sit across from
me and sing my favorite songs under your clarifying breath.
You know I become immensely hurt when you sneer and snicker
behind my back about my childish demeanor, but you do it anyway.
We both know what hurts us emotionally and physically but never
obey the laws of righteous love.
I say we never obey the laws of righteous love because we are more

than just our words; we are more than our whimsical expressions, and we are more than the lifeless spiteful actions we append on each other. We are one.

We are one as a free-flying bird is one with the sky.

We are one as a mountain is one with its indistinguishable high peak.

We are one as doll is one with its oh so clumsy, flimsy body.

We are one as an ant is one with its home, its home an anthill so structured and precisely build.

Now without further ado I must close the curtains on my ceaseless enlightened words of love.

I will say a final encore before I go. I will say we are one in the simplest words I can.

Briana DiVirgilio

An Evening Stroll

Out walking I turned to see
Twilight sneaking up on me
It came on slippered feet
Day whistling a soft retreat
A rustling of the fairy folk
Evening magic did invoke
To the sun I blew a goodbye kiss
Thankful for its warming bliss
Listening to earth's evening song
My heart rejoiced and sang along

Barbara Gorelick

To Live and Die to Live Again

Jesus Christ, the son of God;
  Came down from the heavens above;
But was forsaken by his Love;
  Crucified is where it began;
Giving His Life for all man;
  Stabbed in His heart Jesus would die;
Stabbed in their heart, His people would cry;
  Forseen and predicted by His Father;
Born to a virgin was His Mother;
  Resurrected after three days;
It was His life the Lord would save;
  And to show the people that He gave
His one and only begotten Son
  For a Love, a Love, a Love undone;
To show a Love that no one
  Will ever touch or ever feel;
To ever see what is real;
  To live and die, to live again;
To live and die for all sins;
  To help us love, to help us win;
Everlasting life, to be born again;

Marvin Trujillo

This poem became an inspiration to me while writing it. It made me realize how much we take for granted not only in our own life and love, but the life and love of Jesus Christ and His father who died for us, our family, and friends so that we may obtain everlasting life.

To Z***e

You are quite the magnificent illness
Swollen with love and sorrow in my heart
Smiling at the day's stark steady stillness
Beautifully torn apart at your start

Outside the moments in my dreams
Have I seen your aureate eyes
Blesst to stare deep into their seems
Whispering back your silent replies

How much glass was used to make your hair
Raven black and vivid to their roots
A lovely little Siren's snare
For those who choose to go those routes

But beauty is no tome read worthwhile
Until I feel treasured in your smile

Ryan Walker

Growing Up

The summer sun is fading
And the blue skies are graying
The blooming flowers are wilting
and the autumn weeds are taking
The leaves are turning
And the air is chilling
The mud that's been in our eyes is being washed away
and replaced with ice to clear the way
Suddenly the world has lost its soft touch
and replaced with a cold shoulder
Suddenly there is no moon to keep at our back
For all that was good has gone and fallen to the black

Sheila Humphrey

How Doeth Me?

Who am I? I am me
Am I really? I must be
Do I know what I want?
Yes people always speak

Brian Brown

This poem is about how we are easily influenced, how we lose ourselves in the midst of everything. Touching the basis of conformity which affects everyday life.

I Will Give You All

If only my love was true for you, I would have given you all
If the tears fallen from my eyes were not tears of hatred, I would give you all
If only there were a smile on my face, I would have given you all
If life were like a box of chocolates, I would give you all
If only love were thicker than regret, I would have given you all
If your love for our love were true, I would give you all
If only I had an enemy bigger than my love, I would have given you all
If your heart was for me , I would give you all
If only we had a song that played on every station, I would have given you all
If every time we kissed the stars shone, I would give you all
If only your words were my words, I would have given you all
If we agreed on everything, I would give you all
If only you took that bullet for me, I wold have given you all
But you did do everything for me so I shall do everything for you
You gave me all
Now I will give you all

Kamela Abdul Razzaaq

Absent Girl

Play me a song
for the ones with
a few slashed wrists
and a heart on oxygen

i saw her
holding her head high when a lost father
is once again absent-minded

i saw her
sleeping with the enemy when a drugged up mother
gives her room to an unknown face

this brave girl who once carried the whole world on weak frail
shoulders
gave up and sold herself to a disease

to that creature
lurking behind shadows of fashion magazines and nutrition facts

all charisma lost
all emotion drained

this strong girl
withered away into another gaunt face stuck in the crowd
with nothing to offer but her bones and not so clever thoughts
the walls she built up crumbled down leaving the rubbish and chunks
of change behind as she struggled to become the beast she once
dreamed of

Jane McDaniel

For the Sky

In life, death
was nothing.

The eternal future
of origin:
the universe's light hastily
plunging toward us from its end,
and in the end I can say
that I found this world
sufficiently wondrous.

Rosy, unattainable need.
Holy hallucinations, those
anti-psychotic pills will never
return your soul to its shell
from its quest across the great divide.
The soul is without blemish and immortal,
it shouldn't ever die.

It's not my fault I was born.

To merge at last with true reality
after the deathbed, to merge into
earth, water, fire, to
merge with what has hitherto only been
observed. Soon to join that which now
I simply see.

God can do the inconceivable
but He can only do the inconceivable.
And He is not in my imagination
but rather I in His

Joe Churchwell

I am a writer living in Kansas. I am the author of The Fruit of Exile *and have had poetry and short stories published in* Confluence, The Mind's Eye, The Awakening Review, The California Quarterly, *and* Dance Macabre.

One in the Same, Only I'm Feeling the Pain

Lost in my subconscious mind
Searching between truth and lies
As life around me freezes in time

What we had was unique
Something no one can teach
The warm feeling from my head to feet

Lost in my dreams
Not sure what it means
Wondering if it's only me

Is it me who is having this feeling
Not yet am I healing
Or is it you I'm only seeing

I know we are connected
And yes I have wrecked it
Only am I regretting it

Now time to say goodbye
Letting the feeling pass by
Leaving it lost in my mind

Samantha Tamuschy

Earth

Earth is shaking from left to right.
The earth slowly departed in half.
Earth's inner and outer core exploded into a million pieces.
Nothing was left of the earth.
The people on the earth when it departed in half died.
That is how the earth ended by a small earthquake.

Samantha Popoola

The Shore

Love in my heart is a fresh tide flowing
where starlike seagulls soar.
The waves that rise in restless yearning
are forever broken upon the shore.

The sands of the shore are soft and malleable
although this do be it is hard in a way
which you cannot see.
So I say to you be softly to me for you
have already broken me being alike the sands
which does break the waves that lay
upon the shore.

Terrylee Allen

I'll Be the One

The first day I saw you I knew you were the one,
I'll be the one to hold your hands,
I'll be the one kissing your lips
I'll be the one hugging you tight
When you're gone on a tour I'll watch you perform
Singing your heart out letting your emotions out
Smiling at me with your beautiful eyes, making me have butterflies
I'll be the one to hold your hands
I'll be the one kissing your lips
I'll be the one hugging you tight
I'll be the one that will love you until you hate me
I'll be here until you run out of fame
Take you in my arms to keep you safe
Help you out until you're back on your feet
Knowing you have it in yourself the whole time
I'll be the one to hold your hands just 'cause I feel like it
To keep my hands warm when it gets cold
To be able to know I have someone like you to fit my hands perfectly
I'll be the one kissing your lips whenever we meet and say goodbye
To kiss you again is like a dream
To kiss you is missing you every single day
And finally I'll be the one hugging you tight
Because I'll miss you the days you are not here
Hugging you when you're here is a lifetime
I'll be the one who will be there for you forever and always

Dee Xiong

Only One

I would give up the air I breathe
just for you to see
you are the one I need

Every day and every night
I want you to be the one by my side
please tell me the truth
do you feel the same way too?

If only you knew my name
you would feel it too
that I am the one for you
please say this is true!

This yearning is driving me insane
I only dream of you at my side
If I had you
it would be alright
The fire inside would subside
just feel it too

Your dark hair is what I wish
to run my fingers through
sit beside you and play piano
to every romantic song
my heart beats will play along

I've always wanted to run away
but the place I will run to
is into your arms
it's the only place I will be content.

Just tell me that I will be your girl
it's me over the whole world
and I will say it too
that the only one for me
is you

Brittany Wagner

My writing comes straight from the heart. It is weird because there is no filter or block in between my writing and my soul. It helps me let everything inside out, and this poem is just a small example of that. I haven't been able to express myself all my life, but now that I've found writing and books, even music, my world hasn't seemed so crazy. J. K. Rowling is my true inspiration for writing in the fantasy aspect, but sitting Harry Potter aside, all of the personal writing has been introduced because of authors like her who show that nothing is too unusual or interesting in a peculiar way, to be written down and shared with the world. I'm also inspired by my family, my mom and dad especially. Without their support, my writing would not be what it is today.

Grace and Mercy

I turned to the Lord in my trouble; for His mercy I implored,
He built a fortress around me, and camped outside my door.
I am not without my faults; I've failed Him so many ways,
yet His grace continues to shower me; for that I give Him praise.
If He handed me due justice—how could I stand in His sight?
For despite good intentions, I don't always do what is right.
Yet He sees past my failures, my brokenness and my despair,
He never has to question my motives—He already knows what's there.
I've never known such patience, such goodness I can't conceive,
such love so unconditional is hard for me to believe.
I don't understand such affection; I am unworthy as can be,
how can He show me such love when He can see right into me?
Looking back on past breakthroughs, I can't hold back my tears,
He's solved impossible situations and calmed my deepest fears.
He's the God of grace and mercy, He's the God of integrity,
He doesn't see me for what I am but for all that I could be.

Hattie Pickett

Marriage

I tell you these words from the deepest parts of my heart,
I love you and never want to be apart.
If I could right all the wrongs in my life,
The first would be you as my wife.
To do something I said would never again be,
However life without you I cannot see.
A fruitful life we'll have together,
The strength of our love will surely withstand any bad weather.
So these five words I say to thee,
" _____ will you marry me?"
I feel we're both ready for this,
And we'll seal it all with an I do kiss.
My heart and the fight it's given you,
Is filled with the purest of love this is true.
The rest of my life to you I will give,
Only to bring you love and happiness as long as we should live.
Our wedding vows will end all fears,
And bring out all the joyous tears.
Don't keep me waiting, don't make me guess,
Your only answer can be a " Yes!"

Ray Morgan

Idle Now Walking

For the longest time
I wouldn't bother to speak
My negative pride had me choking
Making me weak
I couldn't write my rhymes
and I couldn't show my flow
My tongue was caught
It wouldn't let me so

I looked up to the sky
Waiting praying wondering why
Why couldn't I soar like I was meant to fly
Why are my wings cut just to die?
No this isn't from God
For I'm a child of the most high

God open my hands and help me to write
Write on my heart so I can recite
Recite your word for your glory
This is how He changed my life . . . here is my story

You think life can be tough
I know it I had it real rough
Dreaming about the day when it will come to an end
There's a lifelong lesson God is trying to send

Out from the dark now I'm into the light
My vision was blurred but now I received my sight
My mind was fading in the darkness when I couldn't see
But now I see my potential of who I'm meant to be
Living in Christ I'm washed by the blood
I couldn't change myself but I knew He could
I raised my hand up and gave Him the praise
For the love He's given me over the days

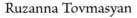

Ruzanna Tovmasyan

Hands

Let me put my hands with yours
open and stretch fingers out

pushing your little hands
curiosity bursting

almost big as yours
I am strong
I am growing

laughter and giggles
covers and paints
the limitless skies

droplets of joy
fills and pours over
emptiness

time travel roller coaster
slideshow begins
moments pass

grabbing the hand
so small
so strong

another travel
begins now

Tomoko Copon

Simple curiosities and observations of a young mind clears up the cobwebs of mental continuum. This poem was inspired by a moment shared with my eight-year-old daughter. Her vivacity and fresh perspectives remind me of the difference between "live" and "alive."

The Presence

Long, thin fingers stretching across the sky,
O'ershadowing the heavens in blackness;
Blotting out the sun with sharp fangs so sly
In a tricky game that would rival chess.
One milky eye watching its trapped prey;
A deadly muzzle swallowing all light;
Hiding under stones and bridges by day
To revive its long-entombed, evil might.
It scratches excitedly at your door,
Waiting to consume all that are afraid;
Greedy for the taste of fear and much more;
Cruel whispers to children at night it made.
Its gruesome territory it will mark,
Does the suffocating creature: the Dark.

Jordan Stickle

Falling

Who knew falling could be this much fun
Falling endlessly toward the sun
Falling backwards
My head in the clouds
Just peace and harmony
Not a bit loud
Amongst the birds flying high
I thought surely I would have died
But I keep falling
I can still breathe
But I'm breathing fast
As you can see
The earth beneath me
A beauty from here
But not as beautiful as the feelings in me
I wonder just when these feelings will end
Then I think, no, I don't want them to bend
I know it must happen sometime soon
As I stretch my hand out to touch the moon
Yet I keep falling,
Falling,
Falling,
For you

Elizabeth Galvan

Diseased Girl

They told me you were gone...
Cardiac arrest:
My heart falters, refusing to beat without you.
Asphyxiation:
Choking on thoughts of you, remembering what we were.
Out-of-body experience:
Seeing all those days we spent, not a care in the world.
Panic attack:
Shaking, tears form behind my eyes, turning memories of you blurry.
Denial:
Tell me it isn't true, or I'll go too!
Coma:
Slowly slipping away, trying desperately to hold on to the feeling of you
against me.
Seizure:
Paralyzed, I whisper your name one last time,
I die with your name forever on my lips.

Selena Tessenear

Take Time to Pray

I was talking with my Sister
just the other day...
She said, "Sometimes I just can't find
the time to pray."

I said , "Sis it only takes
just a minute...
and if you keep putting it off
well then you've done spent it."

You see a minute to God
is like a lifetime I reckon . . .
So if you haven't a minute,
Well then give God a second!

Anyplace, anytime, anywhere,
God listens to your prayers.
Ask and you shall receive . . .
all you have to do is believe.

My sister cried out
Because of her pain . . .
her prayers were answered
her life has now changed.

In Matthew the scripture reads
ask of Thou and you shall receive.
If you find yourself in a bad way . . .
Just remember . . . Take time to pray.

Ronald Kerst

I have always loved writing poetry. "Take Time to Pray" is an inspirational poem that I wrote for my sister. I believe that through my writing I can reach the whole world. I have many awards for creative writing and have been published in several anthologies. Many of my poems have been used as song lyrics.

You Are Loved

When the wind kisses the trees,
then drifts, a light sweet breeze
like your breath upon my cheek
I send a prayer to the Creator above
that you keep safe
and know you're loved.

Heather Hodapp

My husband Chris is a US marine. While in Afghanistan he sustained serious injuries. As he prepared to rejoin his unit, after healing with the help of the Wounded Warrior Project, I wrote "You Are Loved." This is a prayer from my heart to the Creator for my husband. I love you, Chris, more than anyone, anywhere has ever loved anyone else in the history of the world.

You're the Reason

You're the reason I get up in the morning
the reason I brush my hair to look all pretty
And I couldn't imagine not doing that for you

but then you left me here all alone
by myself

but I'll get through
just by thinking of you

Grace Irving

Ever Clear

Life and love
in a dove
like an angel
from above.
You're beauty's face
with silk's touch
and all the things
I love so much.
I hold you dear
and wish you near
for my love
is ever clear.

Chris Hodapp

"Ever Clear" is a relatable spirit, lifting and heart-melting due to its simplicity in expressing the truth of love. There were no drafts, edits, or rewrites because it flowed straight from my heart while thinking of the love of my life. I am not a poet. I am simply a man in love. In 2002 I wrote "Ever Clear" and dedicated it to my girlfriend Heather. She has been my wife for six years now and just as "Ever Clear" was dedicated to her then, it still is today, tomorrow, and always.

375

375 days...

Days of guilt,
days of grief.
Time enough to watch those flowers you picked wilt,
but not enough time for relief.

375 days...

Days of screaming,
days of crying.
Days of hopelessly dreaming,
days of not wanting to keep trying.

375 nights...

Nights of untold tears shed,
nights of restlessness.
Nights of untold scars being bled,
nights of wishing you the best...

375 nights...

Nights of horror,
nights of lies.
Nights of a searing picture of you with her,
nights of living inside my disguise.

375 days,
375 nights.
375 days since you've been away,
375 nights since I've last felt alright...

Emilie Hall

Jumper

Soaring soldier floating in the sky
How does it feel knowing you're about to die
Your jumpchute failed so now you flail
The safety harness seals your doom
The ground is like your tomb
As the strings start to strangle you your bright eyes become dim
You drained a cup that life had filled to the brim
Your mind becomes dull
As the rocks shatter your skull
While the darkness fills your eyes
You swear you can hear your friends cry
"Gory, gory what a hell of a way to die"

Brandon Kimball

Accident

Her train's departure approaches fast,
eliminating any intimate goodbye.

She walks behind me in the shirt I lent her,
holding the present she bought for him.

"It was an accident," she says,
after stepping on the back of my shoe.

Andrew Martin

Alone in My Head

Clear as night,
Dark as day
Still want answers, yet here I lay.

Wanting to break free from the place
I'm in,
Hiding the feelings I have within.

No one really understands me because no one
Really cares
Sick of hiding behind the smile,
I always
Seem to wear.

Dark as day, clear as night
Everything is wrong
Because nothings right......

Trent Beckham

Wall

You build this wall that I can't scale,
Each time I try, I always fail.
You keep me out when I want in,
Each time you push me down again.
You add on bricks to make it higher,
Each time things get even dire.
You hide inside your big stone wall,
Each time you make me crash and fall.
I want to climb up and come inside,
Why huddle down and hide?
I want to know how your castle works,
Why do you bottle up all that hurts?
I want to be there when you're down,
Why not smile instead of frown?
I want to let you know everything is okay,
Why don't you let me in today?

Destiny Brooks

Sands of Time

Tiny grains fall through the hourglass
Each that steals away the hour
Moment lost with every one that passes
Helpless against their power
A cruel betrayer, this miniature thief,
This temptress of lies,
 All succumb, to this harbinger of grief
Tears and heavy sighs
And in the end, with all hope forlorn
When reason has lost its rhyme
The soul will once again be born,
Counting the sands of time

Nikki Sharpe

Life!

We live, we die, life.
What is in between and betrix?
The sun rises and it sets, then darkness sets in.
Is it a good day, bad day, or just a day?
We laugh, we cry, what else is in between?
The sound of the sea, the clouds in the sky, the many things that we see.
Friends, many or few, family members many or few, that we have.
From birth to death,
Seems so short in between!
Some make wise choices in life, some make bad ones!
But life goes on!

Sarah Delatte

Faraway Place

I wander in this faraway place,
A halt in life's continued race.
I bless the grass beneath my feet,
And to the ground that they do meet.
My skin is tickled by the breeze,
My skirt is twirled around my knees,
The birds all sing their lovely songs,
Until it seems they'd right all wrongs.
The flowers' fragrance catches me,
But then strong winds come set me free.
The bees all buzz a calming tune,
The wolves all cry up at the moon.
I wish I had more time right here,
To watch the fleeing of the deer.
But time is what I never had,
I know to leave shall make me sad.
I shan't return in any case,
To wander in this faraway place.

Claire Tollefsrud

And No One Else

He lived his life like a kite,
Flying above everyone that was below him;
Even though he seemed so towering and wonderful
He only held on by a string.

He lived his life like a bolt,
Small and unnoticed inside a brick;
Even though he usually went overlooked
He held the structure of his thoughts together.

He took his life with a kite,
With the string pulled tight across his neck;
The string snapped and so did he,
And everybody knew.

He took his life with a bolt,
Pressing hard onto his wrists;
Alone at night he sat and cried,
And he never dared to care.

Lawrence Uhling

The Best That You Could Do

Almond-shaped eyes
she's the prettiest thing you've ever seen.
Beauty captured in a single photograph
dated 1973.
She had to be in her twenties
before she fell out of grace.
But evidence of her problems
can't be seen on her face.
With the wrong friends beside her
she began to spiral from her high.
Life caught up to her
in the blink of an eye.
And in the same way you watched
her fall all those years ago.
You let the picture drop
onto the coffin below.
Could you have saved her?
You wonder as you lay her to rest.
Could you have done better?
Or was what you did really your best?

Melissa Mui

Healing Garden

I am drawn to the garden each morning to both drink in the present
and escape the past.
Beckoned by its majesty I return over and over, humbly seeking
redemption.
This garden has taught me patience, how to tenderly nurture and
accept the consequences of decline with minimal regret.
Enraptured by its lush splendor, enduring legacy bequeathed to and
from this earth.
Nature's exuberance abounds, crows herald the new day.
These plants do not judge or assess blame and rarely disappoint.
Moss-encrusted patio bricks feel slippery beneath my bare feet.
Here in this garden I am free to shed my facade
Wild, unkempt, bountiful.
Slowly I stoop to gather up the cut flowers which I meticulously
arrange into bouquets.
These blooms are gifts of bribery intended to placate co-workers,
Hoping they will be kind today and not torment me with their chatter.
Memories resonate of a dead friend who loved helping me tend this
garden, taking solace alongside of me.
Shuddering, I silently grieve.
This moment eternally sanctified,
by the cacophony of songbirds
that crescendoes
piercing through
the distant fog.

Joy Feinberg

Not So Alone (the Holocaust)

I sit here waiting.
Ever waiting.
Always waiting.

Crouched in a ball;
Rocking back and forth;
I'm crying, that is all.

"Why" you say?
I have no arms of mother to hold me
No strong hand of father to guide me
No sister, no brother
No other about me.

Eyes wide, frightened; scared
What am I to do?

There's no one around here except you.

A face I've seen in a mirror long ago
So very, very long ago.

Tremors; throbs; convulsions fill me
As my body rejects the food it is given

What am I to do?
When the only person here is you?

Cheybethla Baccia

Falling

When I was falling,
You caught me and held me tightly.
When I was alone with a feeling of emptiness,
You were the friend that filled me with happiness.
When sadness swept through me and my heart shattered,
You comforted me as you scooped up the pieces.
When I cried broken tears,
You wiped them away with a gentle hand.
When I desperately wanted to fly,
You happily gave me your wings.
However, one cold day came,
When you slowly faded away.
I shed tears full of despair,
Because deep in my heart I knew,
We should have been,
Much more.

Brittany Zavala

Carnival

These reels of dreams
[ballerina magic]
Full of color between the cracks

    the flavor of envy

A cast of puppets
    [showtime!]
Witness the revolution

    the pain of public love

Like trying too hard,
Everything falls apart.

Kerri Meredith

This poem "Carnival" is from a series of poems I wrote for my college writing class. Each one focused on a different emotion or image. In "Carnival" I was imagining a ballerina or circus performer being in the "limelight" and failing. I don't write a lot of poetry, more novels and short stories, but I find the best time to write poetry is 2am. Something about that time of night is very inspirational to me!

Missed Love

Every time I think of you my heart skips a beat,
and every time you look at me I fall back off my feet.
Now it is time to forget you and everything we have done.

When I think of breaking it with you my heart falls apart,
but now when I think of you it forms back to one.
I know I need to get you out of mind,
so time and time and time again my heart unwinds
and takes me back to the good old time.

Now I am wishing we are together now.
I am hoping that that will happen someday somehow.
I know you do not feel the same way,
but if you could just remember the good old days,
because every time I think of you my heart skips a beat,
and every time you look at me I fall off my feet.

When you read this poem and you see how I feel,
then tell me what's the big deal.
If you cannot tell me, then think of the good times we shared
when you know I would always be there.
Think of the time when you thought of me your heart skipped a beat
or even the times when you fell off your feet.
Think of the years we could have spent together.

Yeah there would have been an argument here or there,
but if you yourself would think about it, there's arguments everywhere.
When you read this poem and if you have ever cared for me
then think to yourself that could have been you and me.

Tanisha Bennett

This poem came to me because of someone whom I truly cared about, and it's
weird because I was only fifteen when I wrote it and it was something
I had to get off my chest.

Olivia

Fair Olivia, the flower of my heart,
I send to you these lines of love and joy.
Thine eyes glisten and glow like magical art,
Thy angel of my soul, your love is coy.
The leaves of amour descend from the trees,
And fall into the hands of a lovesick lad.
My sympathy for you is like the seas,
Tis love is deep and full of depth, yet sad.
You omit my lust and languish my soul,
For my heart sighs, sorrow after sorrow,
Though I seek upon your grace, it is whole.
Such divine charm will ever have a tomorrow.
Sacred beauty, the angels sing above,
Till eternity, your love remains a dove.

Gabby Catalano

Dearest Love

Dear love, when did your eyes grow cold?
Ice on a frozen pond,
Beneath the gaze of a hurt moon.
Your voice once warm
Now distant, full of despair
Dear love, when did you stop crying?
Rain falling from the heavy clouds
Meeting the earth in a harmonic symphony.
Your touch once gentle
Now a distant memory, gradually fades
Dear love, meet my gaze.
Tell me you still care,
Even if you don't, I do.
The shadows you cast
Must have reason
Dear love, do you remember me?
A sweet, distant dream
Forgotten over time.
Shadows cast upon the earth
Cannot be without first a source of light....

Destinee Howard

*When you love someone, you can let them go but can't watch them walk away
because of the pain. When you are in love with someone it's unbearable to let
them leave but you do and you watch them walk away despite the pain. Good-
byes are not the end of the story but rather the beginning of a new chapter of
our lives. Tears last only a moment, but memories are forever. This poem was
written to commemorate this philosophy.*

Memories

Memories remembered from long ago,
Swirl through my mind like a blizzard of snow.
What brought back the memories from my past?
The ones that I thought I had forgot at long last.
The first day of school I had to walk home alone,
The very first time I got hit by a stone.
The first time I got yelled at by someone so cruel,
The very first time I started crying at school.
Those were some of my memories that were not so great,
But then my bad luck decided to break.
The day I finally went up a grade,
The first day I was no longer afraid.
Suddenly all of my memories were gone,
With the exception of one song.
The song was a wonderful, sweet thing,
It was my favorite song at my wedding.
The song disappears and I am filled with rage,
And then I collapse back into my old age.

Shannon Jackson

What Really Makes the World Go 'round?

What really makes the world go 'round
Is it the passing wind in the atmosphere
Gravity pulling us ever so near
Passionate music swaying us side to side
Or is it children's laughter that makes the earth glide

Shall the answer be made known what makes us spin
Is it the beat of birds wings upon the sky
Or the push of clouds wisping by
May it be the heart of rock-n-roll
Or the cry of a desperate soul

Many have guessed at what turns us round
Science has come up with theories through many a year
The answer to them may seem all very clear
Truly they are lost in space
Wondering upon the prospect of an alien race

What really makes the world go 'round
I sometimes like to ponder
It may be the power of the galactic mysteries yonder
But no, as that may sound true
It is only spun by the love between me and you

Amanda Marx

From a Daughter, to Her Father

Thank you, Dad
For being as understanding as you can
When noticing more boys
Asking to hold my hand

Thank you, Dad
For being in my life
People say we have the same smile
Compliments like that are rife

Thank you, Dad
For teaching me, as a teen
Teaching me about how boys won't always
Understand how much I should mean

Thank you, Dad
For all the lessons I've learned
And for the hugs you've given and will give
Everything you've taught, I think I've earned

Katherine Broyles

The Toddlers' Prayer

God is great, God is good
And we thank HIM for our food.

How sweet it is to hear these words
from little toddlers whose
faith is much clearer than my own.

So, for what I've heard from
God's little angels in sweet accord
Today, I give thanks to you my loving Lord.

Finding joy from the blessings receive
Cheerfully I say, Thank you God
for instilling in me a toddler's heart.

Mary Lou Mackley

When I was still working as a toddler teacher in a Christian pre-school, I was so touched by the innocence of the little children expressing an essential part of prayer which is thanking God. For me, poetry is not merely an expression of emotions shared by the poet, but more of his or her personal experience presented to the reader in an appealing manner. The publication of this humble poem conveys the message that prayer produces faith and our communication to God as His children. I feel truly blessed to have written this poem, and it will be a lasting legacy to my family and friends.

Our Journey

We were waiting for class standing in the hall
I looked over and saw you down the isle against the wall
I didn't know who you were until your friend came over to me
He said you thought I was hot and asked what my response would be
I smiled and told him you and I could chat and see where it goes
What happened from there only the good Lord knows
He sent me you to complete my life and take my hand
He knew that side by side we would stand

We finished high school together, you a year before me
You had signed that line, a soldier you wanted to be
I finished up school while you were gone
I saw you graduate basic and I knew you were the one
The one I wanted to give my soul and heart
I knew I wanted us to never be apart

You came home and we knew what we wanted with our life
Soon after that I was blessed to be your wife
I was nervous and happy to walk down the isle
I walked up to you in your uniform and saw your big smile
I knew from that day forward you had stolen my heart
And it was just you and I, till death do us part
You were a soldier and I your wife
The start of our journey, the start of our life

We were married for two years and decided we wanted more
We were ready and knew a baby we would adore
Maddy came to us so precious and tiny
Oh the fun we had with her always colicky and whiney
As the army moved us around, Maddy grew before our eyes
But don't let her looks deceive you, she's a little monster in disguise
She is definitely a daddy's girl and was from day one
And she has your damn attitude that is never fun

Those five years weren't easy but we made it through a test
We had to make it through the worst to get to the best
God has a plan and made our love strong
The life we made together is where we belong
There may be a few stitches that need to be fixed and resewn
But together we can make our love last even if the future is unknown

Before we knew it, along came another bundle of joy
The Lord blessed us again, but this time with a baby boy
He came into this world with those bright blue eyes
He was so alert and full of energy for his tiny little size
He completed our family, first a little girl, now a baby boy
Our beautiful kids have filled our life with so much joy
You and I babe, we have been through so much
Most things, other relationships wouldn't be able to touch

Dianna Conklin

Dream Big

When you grow older people expect more
When your dreams crash, there's always a way to pick them up from
the floor
Like once you open your eyes and look ahead there you are in the sky
There's always a dream where you can dream as big as you want and as
long as you believe in yourself you will succeed.

Maggie Lau

The Pain of Love

When I tell you I love you, I'm not saying it because I have to
or because I'm trying to start a conversation,
hell no.
It's because life is hard and completely unnecessary,
but you seem to work at life with an ax and hammer till you find gold.

You show me that life is more than pain and suffering,
you can't run from the torture and torment,
because to end your life early isn't going to stop the pain, no,
because when you wake up in your new body all happy and clueless,
the pain's going to come back and slap you right in the face, hard.

So when I tell you I love you, I mean it and nothing can change my mind,
but when life completely beats you up and leaves you stranded,
your clothes and soul torn and shattered,
you bet your ass I'm going to be torn and shattered right alongside you
because the suffering is not worth your life when you're with someone
you love.

But even when I'm completely lost, with hatred and disappointment
pulling at my heart, your words scare all of it away.
When I look into your eyes, all pain is gone.
I see the truth, the lies, and the love.
But when all the dark clouds come back to ruin all that I have,
and when I have given up all hope,
I'll let the darkness take my body, but not without a fight.

Life has to end someday you know.
But this pain, the thing that's killing me slowly on the inside,
will never go away and even with you by my side,
I'm powerless against the torture.
But one day, one special day, I'll build up enough strength to punch life
square in the eye for all the pain it's caused me.
But for now, I fight to stay alive
and if I die trying, just remember I did it for love.

Casey Seligman

I Silence to Beauty

I silence to beauty
as visions of moonlight
and shadows written
by children
soft as death
touched with light.
Can you, such a gentle flower,
truly be mine?

Celeste Sumler

Into Your Eyes

When I look into your eyes, my whole world becomes alive.
When I look into your face, the world becomes a better place.
There is something about your eyes that makes me get hypnotize.
There is something about your eyes that always make me realize,
Why is it that I love you and why is it that I care, why is it that when
I'm with you I feel not one bit of fear.
You wouldn't quite understand what it is I see, in your pretty brown
eyes that shine so beautifully.
When I look into your eyes, it's like I'm lost in a dream and the only
way to wake up is when you close your eyes it seems.
In your eyes I feel comforted, in your eyes I feel strong,
Looking in your eyes is where I feel I belong.
When I look into your eyes.

Samantha Bryan

Egg Shells

Sitting in her broken frame
anger and violence
raging against a fragile child
his hostility and rage fractured her delicate shell
oozing yellow yolk and membranes all over
soiling his hands with her amber blood

Kathy Richmond

This poem is about someone special in my life who inspired me. I write poetry to express my personal experiences, thoughts, feelings, and emotions. I relate them to other experiences. Having the opportunity to have my poem published increases my confidence as a writer and opens me up to a larger realm. I'm very grateful for this. Poetry has been very therapeutic for me.

My Delicate Dreams

As the moon sets in, my mind does too
The pain is over, but the dreams are new
That is where the world can smile
No wars to be started, no tears to be caught
No hate to be spread, no love to be bought
Where flowers can bloom, and bunnies can hop
Where rainbows can shine, and money is no importance
Where hearts are not broken, and love is the only thing spoken
But when the moon gives up, and the sun starts to rise
The tears start to shed once again, because the dream is not alive

Jaelynn Blount

America's Unraveling

Libya
Syria
Same Sex Marriage
Floods
Tornadoes
Permeate the air waves
Riots in the street
Debt ceiling collapsing
Mothers killing children
and nobody's reacting
The world seems numb to the ever decaying morality
as the headlines suck the essence from our souls
God help us!

Frances Dampier

I have always been a champion of the idea of "positive thinking." I live my life by this code. As an educator, I have instilled in my students and my own children the idea of never giving up. Poetry gives me a medium to express my inner emotions. I am thrilled to be included in this publication. Thank you.

Trapped

A small little girl needing to be free
trapped in a body bigger than me.

I tell you to love me and not push away
but the distance gets wider each and every day.

I hate to wake up and see my world again
being trapped is not a nice thing to live in.

People say they love you and try to be nice
but walk away from you with a look as cold as ice.

The ones you trust and should hold you close
are the very ones that will end up hurting you the most.

Annette Smith

From childhood to adulthood, I was physically, sexually, and emotionally abused. As a result of this trauma, my emotional stability was impaired. It wasn't until I experienced counseling in adulthood that I was able to overcome the scars of abuse. My poems reflect my struggles, experiences and feelings. I feel very privileged to have my poem printed in Stars in Our Hearts. *I hope my words will assist others in their journey into wholeness and health.*

Mother

After you left,
My heart turned to stone.
I can hardly feel anything,
Right down to the bone.

You shattered my life,
In pieces it lay.
My heart stopped beating,
The day you went away.

I cried all the time,
Yes, that is true.
But after a while,
My feelings withdrew.

I have no compassion,
No love, no mourn.
After you left,
A new Lindsay was born.

Life has no color.
It is but a dull grey.
I don't want to listen,
I don't care what you say.

You abandoned your children,
You were constantly lying.
Now you're out having fun,
While I sit here dying.

Lindsay Bart

Love of My Life

Searching for the love of my life,
it has been a very long journey, but you, I will find.
Love of my life, you will not be just my lover,
you'll be my best friend for all of my life.
Are you amongst my friends now, or an acquaintance of mine?
Maybe we rub shoulders daily, but we just haven't realized
that you are the love of my life, and I am yours,
just the two of us waiting to shine together brightly as one?
Perhaps we have not discovered each others love light,
because we are too busy,
or maybe it's just not the right time...
life can wear us down, and keep us in a tizzy.
But, no doubt I know that some day soon,
you will see my love light shining bright for you,
and I will see yours for me shining through.
And when for the first time we hold each others hand,
it will be magic, a special feeling we have never had.
I will recognize that magical feeling in you, and you in me,
Oh love of my life, what sweet ecstasy!
Never again shall we feel the pain of loneliness,
because we complete one another, and that brings much happiness.
Love of my life, why is it taking so long?
Well, no matter now, we will find one another,
and that will make our love lights shine brightly together,
not as two, but together we shine as "one" and forever.
To the love of my life...can you see my love light burning bright?
IF you do, then yes, it is ME, the love of your life,
waiting patiently for you, so we can be a part of each others lives.
What a beautiful day it promises to be,
when you and I see our love lights shining brightly,

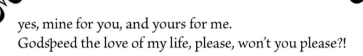

yes, mine for you, and yours for me.
Godspeed the love of my life, please, won't you please?!

Sherry Mays

I have always enjoyed writing poetry but stopped for many years. This poem is one of the first poems I have written in over twenty years. It is very special to me because I have been waiting/looking for the love of my life for many years. I hope everyone enjoys it.

Maria

She is drawn from the kitchen,
from her duties,
by his voice.
Hesitant, uncertain,
she stands in the doorway,
wiping her hands on her apron.
Listening intently, moving closer,
her duties, her sister forgotten.
Sitting down at His feet,
gazing upon Him, not a word is missed.
There is only here, only now.
She knows this:
I am Maria,
I am enough.

Sam Fauskanger

One Heart

My love for you, it's hard to understand how complex it is. To even think the power of it is only created by two hearts. But yet, those two hearts... intertwined in another. Longing for each breath, each brush of another's skin. The warmth of each kiss, warming me up from head to toe. On the neck, the body, the mind, the soul, the heart, your love leaves a mark. Your taste, your voice, the depth of your eyes; how unbearably sweet. You've inspired every dream, every hope, and every wish of mine. Irrevocable, is the definition of my love for you. A dream, yes, I fear you are. Every word, every kiss, every moment of love, leaves a scar. But forever will be kept in my mind. What beautiful light you've given to my life, leading me better than both the Sun and the Moon. My dear, you make an impact on me. You leave me tongue tied.
Take my hand and walk with me.
My finger wrapped around yours, as you spin me around. Forever, our hearts will be bound. Your lips are as tender as our love. Each chance at being alone with you baby, I long for it.
My life is now full of beauty and brilliancy, especially at this hour.
You are the very best part of me. Each feature of yours, permanently sketched in my mind. I look at you, and I fantasize. I'm hungry for your love, let it come, let it arrive, I'm ready. The passion runs through my blood at the thought. You carefully hold my face in your warm hands, and let your lips meet mine.
I hear your heartbeat, its rhythm, in a sequence with mine. We slip into a secret wonderland. Each kiss is as strong as 50 year old wine. We both know what's yet to come, for as long as we've both waited, let the buttons be undone.
I turn my head, across the room, I see the stars shining and sparkling through the window. I've always thought them a beauty. But I quickly turn back to please you.
I hear your breath; feel your skin, the warmth, the closeness your body, crashing into mine. Love is being made, although not by two hearts, but by one that has been bound together by the words of, "I do."

Kaitlyn Mundt

A Phony Smile

I walk into the hospital
terrified of what I am about to see.
I took a glimpse, I was appalled
Who is that I asked? It can't be . . .
But it was . . . he was bald and appeared anorexic
from the chemo.
I assumed,
Or perhaps I overheard those liars talking.
I was eight years old wondering . . .
why my daddy's face was disfigured,
why his thin black hair was falling off in patches
and how melancholy those eyes looked.
I dreaded seeing that phony smile he
painted on his face.
He was trying to fool me to think everything was okay.
But I knew it wasn't, I'm not stupid. Everyone knew.
The more he smiled the more I could see his pain,
pouring out of his defeated eyes.
Desperate to survive.
I called them liars because they tricked me.
They never told me he was going to die.
I hated chemo—it was poisoning my daddy, my hero.
They sent him home and those dumb doctors
put him on morphine to numb the pain.
But who was numbing my pain? Pain was eating my soul,
taking every last bit of me away, leaving me empty and hollow.
No meaning, no purpose
He looked fine, he was getting better.
At least that's what the liars said.
It must have been hard for him to leave his family behind.
Wouldn't it have been hard for you ?
He didn't have a choice,
even if he did his brain was deteriorating.

As those horrible people were putting him six feet under,
my body trembled as an abundance of tears rushed
from my innocent eyes, taking my last feeling of emotion.
And like my daddy
I then painted a phony smile so everyone thought I was okay.

Vienna D'ornellas

I love poetry because it allows me to express feelings and emotions that never got heard. I love my dad and when I saw him die it destroyed me. I was no longer able to feel and was numb to happiness. Thanks to poetry I was able to find and escape. I was able to let all my emotions go and I was able to let go of all the feelings I kept inside my soul. Being able to express myself lead me to have more confidence and motivated me to live to the best of my ability. I am now able to share my story and while it is no longer hidden inside me, it is still a part of me. Whenever I feel defeated, I take a look back at this poem to see how much I have grown, physically, emotionally, and spiritually.

Pain

I hurt inside but don't know why
You just sit back and watch me cry
My feelings are hurt because all you tell me is lies
You don't love me but you won't let me go and fly
I wanna be free but I also want you to love me
"*Love me* as much as I love you"
You promise you won't do the things you do
But no matter what I will always love you
So please love me love me with all your heart
Because if you don't all will shine in the dark!

Tamia Shoats

Poetry has always been my way of expressing life. My poems are not only about my life, but about the things around me and people in my life. Me writing poems are wonderful to me and my family and friends. My poems also describe me and what I do.

Lover's Dance

The slow dance begins
and we spin in circles
like child's top.

There is passion in our touch
and lust on our lips.
Our hearts beat harmoniously together.

Our body's rhythm matches
the tempo of the piano
and we can't avoid getting
lost in each others gaze.

We are lovers until the song ends,
we part longing for our song
to be played again.

Zachary Vasey

The Dying Children

While all the children die
You won't even cry

For their poor little soles
With empty bowls

Who died in vain
With all their pain

Look them in the eye
And try to say goodbye

Go ahead
Turn your back on them

Pretend they're not real
And that they don't feel

Pain and sorrow like we do
And they don't need a shoe

A shirt
Or a skirt

Afraid of life
Only release a knife

Death is what's known
And it hears their moans

Filled with sorrow
Life no better tomorrow

They live in holes
No better than moles

They can barley breathe
With no one to grieve

For them
While it has been

A hard life to live
With nothing to give

But they are strong
Through their life hard and long

They never feel loved
Always pushed and shoved

But they do matter
Even with their lives shattered

Some people don't want to believe
But not me

Because someone has to care
And always be there

They need to be thought of
So rise above

Please be smart
And keep them in your heart

They are people like you and me
So treat them like a human being.

Alina Wetterau

This I Promise You

A love so rare and true,
I will do my best to
make all your dreams come true.
This I promise you!

I love you with all my heart,
Soon we will never be apart
Then soon I will say a vow from my heart,
Take your hand and place a golden band,
And say I do
This I promise you!

And when we are old,
we will look into each others eyes,
And still realize with ever glance
And thank God for this love that is so rare and true
This I promise you!

Kevin Peace

Your Picture

Your picture makes me smile;
It also makes me cry.
I only wish that I had known
and got to say goodbye.
So many things I want to say
so many tears I cannot hide,
for half of me went with you
that very day you died.
You were always there to make me laugh
when my world had fallen apart;
I only wish that you could help me now
and mend my broken heart.
I'll keep your memories with me
to guide me through each day,
and when I look upon the heavens
I know I'll be okay.
For someday I will see you
and hold you once again,
and take a stroll through Heaven
with you, my brother, my friend.

Lacey Sager

Daddy's Little Girl

You watched me grow older
You held my hand through my pain
You never left my side
No matter how hard the rain
You watched as I've changed
From a little girl to a teen
As I moved from Barbies to cell phones
And everything in between
You've watched me laugh
You've watched me cry
I miss your old self daddy
It hurts as I watch you die
I'm scared beyond belief
I know Mom is too
It seems like every day it's getting worse
I don't want to lose you
I know we don't have the best relationship
And were always in another fight
But you're still my childhood best friend
Who would hold my hand through the night
I remember being daddy's little girl
I remember exactly how much I've always looked up to you
And I know I hardly ever say this anymore
But, Dad, I promise I love you, too.

Dusti Hargis

I Love You

I love you because you first loved me.
I love you because you came to me when I needed you most.
I love you because you are all I hoped for.
I love you because you are my Joy.
I love you because you mean so much to me.
I love you more than you'll ever know.
I love you because I need you.
I love you because I depend on you.
I love you because it's time for me to tell you so.
Now you know I love you so.

Coleen Fountain

This poem was for a person who inspired me to write. I love to write and hope people will enjoy it.

The Beggar

A beggar, sat dusty, on a road to the city
his hat in the dirt, with the wind's steady blight.
Not a token, a grain, or an emblem of pity,
the hat remained empty all night.

His demeanor quite flat,
as the sun hid its face.
Just beggar, and hat,
in the vast void of space.

Payden Neumann

When I Knew I Loved You

When we touched for the first time, I was afraid to kiss you
When we kissed I was afraid to hold you
When I held you I was afraid to hold you too tight
When I held you tightly I was afraid to let go
When I let go I was afraid I would never hold you again
When I left I was afraid that was the last time I would ever hold you
When I thought that was the last time I would kiss you, hold you, or
see you
That is when I knew you reached my soul, but now that I am so close
to you, I'm afraid to lose you!

I just cannot describe how it feels
I am so excited when you walk in the room
I love the way you take care of me when I'm sick
I love the way we laugh together
I love the way you hold me
I love the way you make love to me

I am so glad to have met someone so special as you
My heart is feeling something I never knew

Grace Kelly

Poetry has always been where I can express my feelings. I write poems that are truly a part of my life. This poem was written because I fell in love.

I Am Your Mama!

You came into my life when my son married your mommy. As a baby I held you close. We sat in church and sang songs, your little voice echoed above all others. I closed my eyes as my heart soared with the promise of being there for you, "I am your Mama!" You grew so fast. I cherished the bedtime prayers, the silly songs we'd make up, to the walks on the beach and eating blueberries while crawling like lions on the floor—you were amazing! Every moment was one to love you! Wow, "I am your Mama!"

Then life attacked your tender little family. I don't really know what happened, but no one fought for it. Your little family tore apart and hearts were broken. Days turned into weeks, weeks into months, then one night I got to talk to you on the phone. You said, "Mommy says you're not my mama anymore." Oh my voice echoed what my heart promised long ago, "I will always be your Mama." Two and a half hours we talked, sang songs, looked at the same moon through the phone . . . Both getting sleepy, you didn't want to hang up, you didn't want me to go. I said, "Mama will stay on the phone till you fall asleep." A few minutes passed and your little voice called out, "Mama are you there?" "Yes, Mama's here." As you sighed and sleepily said, "Okay Mama," my heart once again confirmed that promise of long ago . . . "I am your Mama."

Osherrie Bowman

Nature's Dance

The scorpion dances lightly,
With the twist of his tail,
As the tarantella seems to mambo,
By the fence's wooden rail.

The red fox bucks and wings,
His plumb held up high,
As though rock and rolling,
Across the ruby sky.

Two fawns in the meadow,
White spots appear to glow,
A cotillion in the grass,
Coordinating a fast tango.

The grace of the bobcat,
Reels across the way,
A cottontail's cha-cha motion,
As he jumps the promenade.

This choreography of nature,
Under the sun's spotlight,
Reflections of His glory,
And creative power and might.

Monte Hardin

Divine Diversity

There are people who live in caves
just think of the money they save.
They never work just roam the land
reaping from nature what they can.

Sip cedar cider from a cup
Runs for their cave when storms come up.
And thank God for blessings of life,
allows Divine Lead to repeal strife.

Their focus' on the inner self,
learns from the Bible on the shelf.
They study creations' natural flow
while selfless service—yearn to know.

Streams provide hygiene, water and food;
The way they live some think is crude.
Their devout peaceful way from strife
Helps grasp divine purpose for life.

All creation's a written poem.
They are God's children, He cares for them.

Troyce Leona Tollison

My life love is poetry. This poem shows God's nature covers a multitude of subjects and embodies all living. It's significant because all life's enraptured in its ambiance. It's a steward of beauty that differentiates the kinds, sorts and types of its environs. Its range is vast. Its law is kept orderly. Its disposition and temperament exposes quirky instincts and the primitive state of the universe while it rejuvenates and captivates all living. More of these poems are in "Beautiful Poems Beautiful Places with a Different Twist." Life is nature. All things living are all things inclusive. Nature.

Human

In bloodthirsty requital, we tread our foes,
Crush beating hearts, thrust deadly blows.
Our claws are clad as iron lords, are cursed as gripping mortal swords.
The feet, the lowliest of the whole, sprint far ahead on burning coal.
And though they bite the dust each stand,
Their pride competes with the walk of man.
Our eyes pierce far beyond their sight to grow on greed in green delight.
Heads puffed with truth and filled with wrong.
Men never look down till on another man's song.
The world holds merely one, and reality lost,
Imagination too true, but sworn to be tossed.
Divisions, Divisions, Divisions entice. Hands once joined now drip red,
Feet that carried cruelly thrust advice.
A curse so real gives blind delight, starves fatted cows, weakens every might.
The men and women shatter glass, and sight is lost in reflections that pass.
An earth of deadly tongue and deed craves life in satisfying need.
But must untie the bonds of night and share demand of common fight.
So take my hand once more Lost Friend.
Drop battered sword, feet's race to end. Hearts mend your glass, Heads
understand. The fight we fight together, the common duty: Human.

Natalie Riebel

This poem was inspired by every one of us in this world who share a common bond as humans. It holds a message I hope to share with everyone of the opposition and hate the world shows towards those within it but also of the hope that we all may have if we work together and recognize our common bond as humans who must fight the common fight every day for all those in need. We must recognize this bond, tear down our defenses of pride or selfishness, and begin making the whole world a better place, human by human.

Inside Out

They say I'm on the inside
and yes, they call me friend
but if that's so, then tell me why
I'm always at the end
I'm inside, but inside what?
for hell can't be this bad
yet friends, we're called, supposedly
why does that make me sad?
They care for me, or so they say
yet they can't really care
for if they did, then one would think
they'd see me standing here
They say I'm in, and that we're close
so tell me why they've lied
if this is in, and this is friends,
I'd rather be outside

Batsheva Tendler

I Live

As I set in the palm of God's safety, I venture out into the world
I feel as though I have taken my first breath, like a small child just born
Yearning to learn of new things, while my past still teaches me
As my two entwine together, I walk on an untouched mountain
The smell of fresh flowers, a warm breeze, and the sounds of the bees
It feels so refreshing, brisk, and warm as the sun lightly warms my skin,
I smell the sweet scent of honeysuckle and hear the sounds of peace

It feels so good, God, so why do I hesitate? Is it because of what I
know, or because of what I don't, Lord? I know I must go, Lord, take
me in your palms, Lord, take me there
Lead me up the mountain of my unknown place and take me to where
you want me to be

I know you will allow it to rain, so I feel the wetness and the cold
I know you will allow the lightning to strike me, so I feel pain
I know you will allow me to live and have this entire mountain

I am cold, Lord, from the wetness of the rain, I hurt from the lightning
that has struck me, Lord, the bees are stinging me, Lord
Oh the pain of this mountain, Lord, it hurts
My skin is no longer warmed by the sun, my body quivers from the
cold of the rain and my skin burns from the sting of the bees
I'm so afraid, Lord, like a child just born. What do I do, Lord, help me!

As I walk into the palms of your hands and feel the warmth of the sun,
smell the sweet scent of honeysuckle and hear the sounds of the bees. I
thank you, Lord, for letting me live, feel, and learn. Thank you for life!

Kim Rademacher

Kathy and Kathy

A coincidence and family friends brought them together,
Two little girls that would be best friends forever.
They're still very different but also the same,
In many ways and not just their name.

From Lagoon to movies to Cowabunga Bay,
They always make the best out of their day.
Together they have gone through quite a lot,
Like falling off a couch and being threatened with a pot.

At sleepovers they play and have lots of fun,
With balloons, games, and pictures of the sun.
They do things with their own little flair,
But are always laughing and gasping for air.

Who have been best friends since they were two?
Well of course Kathy Liu and Kathy Liu.

Kathy Liu

For You I Would

My legs are weary, tired, and weak
ahead lies the road, I'm not yet at the peak
The air is sharp it pains my skin,
the darkness outside, I can feel from within

My mind is numb, my soul is lost
I must find my way, no matter the cost
My body is blistered, anguished, and torn
through loathe, fright, and dread, further effort is born

My heart is the buttress that keeps me upright
its depth and its memory gets me through the night
When the sun finally rises, and reaches its height
it brings peace to this man, the end now in sight

When I realize my potential, despite pain and fear
I will tell you the reason, I need you to hear
When I struggle, when I fight, as I know I should
You are that reason, for you I would

John Lauze

La Di La Di Dah

La di lah di dah and
so ticks the clock
I got all the time in the world
as the world continues to turn
My existence will carry on
So carry on, please do carry on
Once more the sky
will swallow the sun
Giving birth to the dark
and just as before
the dawn will come
bringing along the sun
to draw back the curtain
of the night to reveal
a new day's breath
all without you or your approval
so la di lah di dah
the world shall carry on
whether you wish it to or not
so what do you think of that?
Oh please share with me your mind?
I have nothing better to do
than to hear your words of iodine
so la di lah dah
I got nothing but time to kill
I got two open ears and
a closed-off mind
so go ahead give me a try
I've figured out that my
existence, nature and time
all continue just fine
without you having to share your mind
or giving your yes or your no
or I told you so
So la di lah di dah

Abbygail Mark

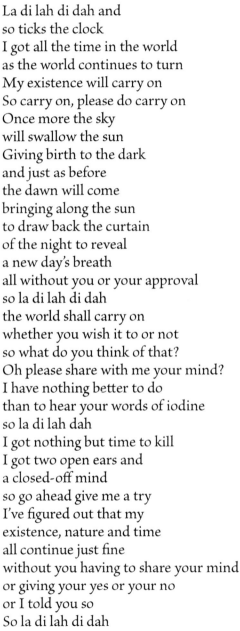

I Believe in You

There I stood with honor looking back at my new life
this man of courage, strength and pride . . .
To defend my freedom in war if right.
"War"—an act unthought of, for in my heart our land was free;
As I began to fall in love with you
I saw my future . . . You with me.
Here I stand still falling, though with honor, more with fear...
For war is sternly calling you
too far away from here.
"Thousands of lives destroyed" by "faceless cowards" lives are lost.
"America attacked" by who will now
Quote "pay the cost."
Of the United States Marine Corps, Corporal Harper... "I salute you."
Go off and fight for liberty, for as you say
"You choose to."
My fear is simply selfishness for me to be alone.
Without you I am weakened . . . You are my strength
your arms my home.
Before you go, I'll say a prayer:
"Dear God, please walk beside him. If danger threats his coming home
please be a shield to hide him." Amen
As you go, if you should turn around, you will see my head is bowed;
But know this—I believe in you,
You are my heart . . .
And I am proud.

Tricia Harper

*Poetry has been a part of my life for as long as I can remember. As a little
girl I used to write for my church. I wrote this poem for my husband after
9-11 when our World Trade Centers went down. I wanted him to know
I believed in him, I was praying for him, and that I love him. Thank God
he made it home eight days after I gave birth to our first child. He is now a
staff sergeant in the United States Marine Corps Reserves and to
this day I salute him.*

From Illusion to Reality

Words some say are an illusion of the image they want to portray that on a rare occasion ends up becoming reality.

No matter what happens reality is to mean what you say and say what you mean . . . for better or for worse until death do us part

How can you say you love me
When you were the one that went out behind my back!
Setting the illusion in my head that you loved me

When in reality you lied to me throughout the entire time!

Is anything that anyone says reality anymore?

How can people be trusted when no one knows the difference?
Or the meaning of illusion or reality!

An illusion when speaking is a fantasy that is painted through spoken words, reality is the truth spoken of a situation and it is what it is.

What is real anymore?   I'm not sure but one thing I know is real is the love we've given each other throughout these years.

I don't ask you for much the one thing I do ask you for is the reality of respect. Don't paint the illusion of what could be, paint the reality of what there is.

I know it's been hard for us but I promise to make a reality of my words and my actions as long as God allows me. So that we may be able to eventually live the illusion that was once painted in both of our heads and this way we may travel from illusion to reality.

Zigmia Cruz-Fusaro

Poetry is an expression of the pain and life lessons learned throughout the years. Inspiration for my poetry is to hopefully encourage and be able to reach out to just one person. "From Illusion to Reality" was based on a relationship I had. Now only a great but true friendship remains.

Summer Fun

I've traveled far and wide
With a road map at my side.
I've been to places like Disney Land,
And at Astroworld listened to a band.
I went white water rafting down the New River,
And swimming in the Atlantic, it made me shiver.
I rode the Beast at Kings Island,
And worked a bit at Adventureland.
Busch Gardens was a great place to be,
Bok Tower was a beautiful place to see.
The Creation Museum was awesome,
Quite an eye opener and then some.
Now Pensacola air museum is a place for me,
Maybe even a chance for the Blue Angels to see.
There are a lot of places to observe,
Some just may be around the curve.
Just pick a place that's fun,
But, you must walk, don't run.

William Wheeler

America Voted

Nobody read and nobody wrote
Like the year 2008 presidential vote
It is the mystery that Americans got
A phenomenon that ears caught
A tangible fact that nobody thought
From within or from the remote
It was for this reason that others fought
Because of their struggle and a huge effort
Here it is we have witnessed what they brought.
Peoples of the world recorded a great history
The history that was recently made in this country
The history that was in no one's memory
Indeed it is a fabulous mystery
For the United States, it is a humongous victory.
As peoples of the world listen
Americans taught a great lesson
By opening the strongest button
Absolutely not all of a sudden
But after life sacrificing jobs were done
Jobs which will never be forgotten.

Kinati Woyessa

Visions

Visions,
behind closed doors of sleep
like some shattered mirrors we keep
tucked away; sharp, splintered shards
more painful than the waking hours
of day we reap.

Is this the plague inside of man
that tempts his works and slight of hand
Changing carbon dust to stones;
diamond mines and vaults of bones,

Immortal dreams of steel to steal?
(as if his blood and flesh were real!)

Yet, finally, when his days grow old
his visions purged of weighty gold
and he lay naked in the Earth
his Maker's dust alone
Rebirth!

Pam Barletta

It has been my gift from God—this yearning to lay down words attached to thoughts, ideas, internal revelations, lost and found emotions, growth spurts from love and other strange places—all translated into picture images meant to be shared.

Dear Vince

How do I say I'm sorry to my first-born son?
How do I explain to him the awful things I've done?

From the first day he was born, his body went through much.
He shivered and shook and jerked away from just the slightest
touch.

Coming off of heroin was very hard for me,
and now the pain of addiction in his body was easy to see.

Watching his body struggle inside a glass cocoon.
How could a mother do this to the life inside her womb?

And growing up with me has not been easy for you.
I've screamed, yelled and pushed you away, so in peace my drugs
I could do.

As a little boy and growing up, I didn't see the harm.
That you were watching mommy put a needle in her arm.

Is there something I could say to let me in your heart?
To let you know I love you and make a brand new start.

I know that Vince you find it, very hard to believe,
that I love you oh so very much, a notion you can't conceive.

So how do I say I'm sorry for all the things I've done?
I've only mentioned just a few, but the list goes on and on.

And each and every night, I wonder where you are.
I pray to God to keep you safe and free your heart from scars.

So here are words from my heart, the very least I can do.
If only I could echo them across the fields to you.

So please forgive me for as a mom, I know the wrongs I've done.
I've put you through a living hell, things a mom shouldn't do
to her son.

Nancy Kassees

Lay Me Down

Lay me down on a bed of green grass
So that I may feel the warm summer breeze
Flow gently across my furrowed brow;
Let me feel the power of the golden sun
As it warms me to my very soul.

Lay me down with my ear to the wind
That I might hear the rustle of the leaves
As the trees sway in the soft summer breeze;
Hark! Do you not hear the sweet melody
Of the lonely whippoorwill?

Let me gaze into the heavens above
That I might see the heavenly lights
As they twinkle in the darkening sky.
Lay me down that I might at last find
Everlasting peace.

Oh, lay me down that I might see, feel,
And hear all of God's wonders of life;
Lay me down for my time is at an end.
So, lay me down and weep not for me,
For my dear Lord is calling me home.

Bobby Fassler

Seasons of Change

Roaring rapids, falling rain,
Water washes all the pain.
Splashing ponds, falling snow,
Water swiftly starts to flow.

Sunshine falls bright and hot,
It was raining now it's not.
Children play out all day long,
Singing happy Summer songs.

Leaves turn from green to brown,
Leaves start to fall down.
Temperatures drop every day,
"Put on a jacket" my mother would say.

This time of year is best of all.
This time of year lets snow fall.
The sky turns all dark and gray,
But that doesn't mean you still can't play!

Hannah Ng

What Is Love?

The something that comes from within that cannot be explained
The honor of a friendship that blossoms and grows
The tenderness of words and the touch of a hand

Hope of steadfast dedication to the one of adoration
Hope of warmth infused with passion for one another
Hope of pleasing the one in high regard

Trust to the point of no return
Trust in the flame of desire
Trust in the one that is held dear to your heart

Dedication continuing throughout endless time
Dedication to the one who is deserving
Dedication to the one who is cherished and appreciated

Affection that is held isn't the heart everlasting
Affection that is heard in the voice as well as in the soul
Affection that is felt to the core

Respect one as you respect yourself
Respect the recognition of change
Respect the rights and ideas of the one you a have eyes for
Respect one and always expect it in return, always

Sandra Moschiano

One

We are one
Under the sun
From the Earth we came
One and the same
Let us join, with great joy
Together
Forever
Every girl and every boy
For we all dream
So I deem
We are one
Under the sun
We'll join in unity
Under our great tree
Simply because
We are one
Under the sun

Chanamon Lerdnitiseth

The Last Mortal Day

Standing on a white beach, my toes curling in the sand,
it wasn't that long ago you held my heart in your hand.
Staring at the ocean with a smile on my face,
it is so gentle, so lovely, this place.
The waves come and go, they twirl and twist,
reaching for land with a flip of their wrist.
The sun it is setting, the sky is so blue,
in the wind I can hear it . . . a distant "I love you."
I left without warning, with weight on my heart,
I felt it was better if we were apart.
Although you love me, although you care,
most times it felt as if you were not there.
The world was so wicked, the people were too,
so it was best that I had left you.
They hated different and tore it apart.
They came with their pitchforks, their knives and black hearts.
They said, "Our god hates you; you will burn in hell."
Sooner than later my screams rang like a bell.
They grabbed my arms and twisted me down,
twisted so hard I fell to the ground.
They punched and they kicked with all of their might,
until a pool of blood was clear in my sight.
They screamed you're not pure in the eyes of our leader,
look at this guy . . . look he's a bleeder.
They carved with their knives . . . carved into my chest,
I tried to fight back—I gave it my best.
They looked down at me with anger and hate,
and then I saw it, a tall pearly gate.
Their voices did fade with each step I took.
I did not turn back, not one last look.
The night sky turned golden, the cement to sand,
and I woke up with a sword in my hand.
The pain was gone the wounds were too.

And then I heard it—the first I love you.
My clothes once tattered, bloody and torn
fell from my body—I was reborn.
I stood up and noticed the strangest of things . . .
a shadow behind me. Look I have wings.
Dedicated to every man, woman and child
who has lost their life due to gay hate crimes.

Joshua Donley

Butterfly

Butterfly dragonfly fly away,
when the time comes we'll be home again.
One day at a time is all it takes,
but eventually it'll be great.
So butterfly dragonfly fly away
at last we're inseparable.

You ask me why I love you so
I simply say butterfly dragonfly fly away
I love you now until the end of days,
with mended hearts our love entwined
I love you this much my love's divine.

Heather Wells

Free Fallen

why is everything so open
like sirens ringing in my ear?
i fall to the ground.
i collapse from fear.
i see your lifeless body
laying on the ground.
i fought with myself—
you didn't really drown.
the police tell me to stay away
but i can't,
not today.
i think to myself
"if only i was here
i could have stopped you."
now i lay in bed
listening to the sirens
echo in my head.
I can see the firetrucks
rush straight to the scene;
everything's still so clear,
your face was unexplainable.
the pain you had, it showed.
the scars you made
make me now understand all the lies.
your hair lost color—
a beautiful brown
to an empty white
then everything goes black.
i don't see your face anymore.
i don't see your lifeless body
or the people,
the lake . . . .
i see black.

i get scared to think you're gone.
your voice fills my mind
and air forced in my lungs
i awake.
my eyes see nothing;
am i really awake?
i hear a voice
but it's not yours.
"i'm sorry, miss,
but we lost your friend."
the words choked me—
no air to breathe.
the last thing i ever saw
was your lifeless body,
an empty white
painful body.
i think again
"if i was there
i could have saved you,
i could have saved you from yourself."
but
i was there,
i was just too late
and never again
will i leave.

Courtney Kurtz

Middle School

Middle school, the taunts, the teasing,
who's dating who. The clothes you wear,
and oh they care,
the stares they give you when
you don't meet the expectations
of new fashions and trends.
Tomboys like me, considered gay and freaks,
just couldn't be accepted.
Sitting at lunch while others gathered in a bunch
to be part of a social circle,
Oh how I so wanted to belong.
But I knew it wouldn't be long until I moved on,
and all of this would end.
The one day I would get out of bed
and see myself acceptable to the dreadful
ways of middle school.

Karianne Rogerson

Baseball Is Life

You got your hot dogs,
popcorn and pretzels,
and your six dollar beer.
The crack of the bat,
it's the sweetest sound,
you'll ever hear.
Come on out to the ballpark,
never mind your wife.
Let's drink some beer,
curse the other team,
'cause baseball is life.

Andy Deason

The writing bug touched me when I was a mere child, and the world came to life in my writing. My two published books, My Life *and* My Poetry and the Dog Pen, *have become a dream come true. I am currently writing two more. I am having the time of my life having poetry readings and comedy shows, anytime and any place I can. Thanks so much for the thrill of having a poem published in this anthology.*

Perfectly Blinded

Do you ever look up into the sky
see a star flying by
you make a wish
because you think it will come true
and what your wishing
has always been you

You may not see it
but the wish is there
you wished you were perfect
without a scare

you look in the mirror
you're still the same
you thought your wish bounced
because nothing changed

but you were always perfect
you just couldn't see
you were perfectly blinded
with what you wanted to be

Sophia Villarreal

*Poetry is life! Every time I write a poem it's normally about me and my life.
But it's not only about my life; it's about life in general. What I see, hear, even
a picture makes me want to write poetry. I'm glad I have this opportunity to
share one of my favorite poems with other poets and readers. While writing
this poem I thought about everyone who wishes they were different from who
they really are. To those people , we need you in this world. Everyone is their
own person. So be happy with who you are.*

Love Is . . .

Love is a flower in the spring
Love is the reason birds sing

Love is a rainbow in the sky
Love is a colorful butterfly

Love is a beautiful summer day
Love is what shows us the way

Love is the ocean so calm at night
Love is a star that shines so bright

Love is going to last forever
Love is why we belong together

Angie Clifford

The Voice I'll Never Forget

Listening to you, your voice full of compassion and dreams,
you sing your songs and we hear what they mean.
The lyrics reach to open minds, open hearts, and open souls.
The rhythm of the music replaying in our minds everywhere we go.
We think of success, your name comes to mind.
We think of love, and you are what we find.
Your music overwhelms us, it brings us all to tears.
Your music makes us forget our regrets, our past, our heartbreaks, our
fears. They fade away to the back of our mind
as we fall more and more for you every time.
I hear you asking for that one all day girl,
and for you to be mine, would be like having the world.
In the palm of my hand to hold on to my whole life,
to have you with me, I just couldn't name a price.
Your style is original; it's all your own.
You never have to worry about being alone.
Your fans are always behind you, no matter where you go.
We love and support you, for everything you are,
you're not just another singer, you're our shining star.

Autumn Mills

Inside the Mind of a Flower

I can't grow without tender loving care.
Dig me up, don't you dare!
I need the ever refreshing rain to survive.
The ever refreshing rain is my friend.
Without it, how could I begin?
But first, I must be placed in the dirt, you see!
You can do it! It doesn't require an expert, believe me.
It requires patience, to see me reach my full potential.
When all these steps are done, including the ever glowing sun.
Oh how beautiful, oh how delightful, I become.
I am wonderful to the eyes, hands, and nose.
Stand back and enjoy the view.

Reginald Gentry

Poetry and writing in general is all part of me. God has birthed it in me. I write all types. I'm a songwriter as well. "So a man thinketh, so is he." I lay down, I get up thinking about poetry. Writing is me. I wake up thinking poetry. I lie down thinking about poetry. Poetry comes to me in my sleep. Inspirational poetry is my main interest. This poem is about how a flower would respond and relate to us if it could speak. Even a flower needs special attention. God bless.

when i see you

when i turn in the hall all i see is you
your eyes, your hair, your pain
i know what you feel
i can't bare to even think about the feelings
that rush through my body and out my scars
those are it—my feelings
my cold, permanent, memorial feelings
that will now live with me for all eternity
I can't stand to look any longer for if I do
I am afraid that I might see myself in you
but I cannot look away now you've caught my stare
and now everyone has vanished into the darkness
leaving only us two behind
I can't breathe
it's like we have our own little secret now
I love it
I look at your eyes and see a sea of blue
but then when I look in your eyes
and I see nothing but a desperate soul trying to escape
please, someone pull me out of this black sea
please

Marissa Arroyo

Common Sense

It is not proof, but it makes sense for us
To hold the door for someone who's behind.
Do not jump out right in front of a bus.
Surely don't let the drug mess with the mind.
Please throw away the milk when it goes bad.
Turn off the lights when they are not in use.
Know the difference between mom and dad.
Do not confuse discipline with abuse.
To be funny and then to be a jerk
Is going from friendly to so shallow.
When to sleep, when to eat, and when to work
Are very important for one to know.
But do not keep these "secrets" to yourself,
Please pass the knowledge to somebody else.

Michael Cruz

Cooling Comfort

I cry for the love that has left me so
Whose soft sweet lips cannot further utter my name
The one whose gaze shall never lie upon me

Yet, when she is near it all becomes clear
That the constant comfort of her cooling soul
Can ease the burning of my broken bruised heart....

Alexander Campozano

Riding in the Light

A knight in shining armor
Riding in the light
With no fright
A little lover
A cover
 Little sex shield
Healer, feeler
Helping all to stay happy
Fighting for freedom
Until the light dims at night
A knight in shining armor
Riding in the light

Alyssa D'amico

What Is Faith

FAITH!
Follow your heart desire
Allocate your time wisely
Institute your-self regularly
Think twice before take action
Health is the ingredient to life journey.....

Tri Dang

In the Dark

In the dark there is sadness and crying because you are not in my life...

With you there was happiness and light so why did you leave me in the dark all by myself...

Please come back because I don't want the darkness to close in...

I want to see light so just come back because I am in the darkness waiting...

Trista Yawn

Poetry is new to me. I always wrote down my feelings in songs until I realized that poetry is music without the instruments. This is a new experience that I hope to continue.

Sweet Baby

The day you were born was such a beautiful day
I felt so much love
Love that was here to stay
I could never imagine a love so strong
You made my life complete
God created this miracle
This miracle of mine
Immediately there was a bond
I will love you forever
Unconditionally
Sweet baby of mine

Debra Haynes

Expressing myself through poetry gives me a chance to write about my children and what means so much to me in my life. Sharing with others is a privilege to behold.

The If Only

I will rise above the clouds:
See the world like a jewel below;
Sing among the stars;
Explore the universe.

Even if only in a dream
I will see what no one's seen;
Do what no one's done;
Be what no one's been.

I will rise above the clouds,
Out of the strife and confusion:
Leave it all behind,
Explore the unexplored.

Even if it is just a dream
I will savor every second,
Relish every choice,
Cherish every feeling.

I will rise above the clouds:
Walk among the stars;
Leave behind my fears;
Explore the if only.

Randi Dukes

My Middle Son Is Forty Today

He's 40 today—middle child of mine,
Been on my mind lately all the time.
Need to write about things, help him understand.
I know for certain he's a very good man.

Handsome and smart with a capable hand,
Skills and speed, would help you if he can.
I love him a lot—always did, always true.
Am sure he lives by the Golden Rule.

Want him to prosper, forgive and smile.
Sadness and pain he had to live with awhile.
Hope he's happy, loved, and loves back too.
Is with somebody who is worthy and true.

Funny little boy who was cute as could be,
Sadness since the breakup of our family.
Latch key kid with too few rules,
Grew up too soon with too few tools.

Like mother, like son, we are both so needy
For love, security and just too greedy.
Sorry for mistakes I made were many,
Just a child myself and not very steady.

Still I loved him a lot, maybe best for awhile,
Made me laugh and tried to make me smile.
Considerate and kind then beyond his years,
Seeing his mom so often in tears.

Wish I'd made a lot of different choices,
Would be close enough to use our voices.
To say those things that should be heard,
"I'm sorry. I love you and wish you the best in the world."

Advice he won't take, not from me.
If he did, he would try and finally succeed.
Forgive and remember the good not the bad,
For life is better when you aren't mad.

Unhappy myself most of my years,
Finally getting away from some of my fears.
Still need to mature more myself a bit more.
Hope soon I'll be happier than ever before.

Meanwhile I wonder and wish and pray
My son would have a wonderful day.
Be loved and happy and full of good cheer
And hope that the next is a very good year.

Karen Mueller

*My thoughts tend to rhyme in my head when I'm sad. Might I put them on
the computer or use pen and pad. Now a widow, trained in technology gone
by, while I watched my father and then my husband die. Life's been a struggle
for me and mine. I think sometimes that's why I rhyme. Divine madness,
indeed. Divine insanity, perhaps. I'm with Plato and Socrates thinking that.*

Tree

There she is swaying in the breeze,
arms stretched out as pretty as you please.
She'll bow and sway but she won't go away.
You can watch her each and every day.
You can love and enjoy her—just come and see,
but she can't be yours—she was born to be free.

Lovely to look at—a sight to behold
as her arms reach upward, even when it's cold.
Arms that will shield from heat and cold
she seems more lovely as she grows old.

More and more graceful through the years you see
the name of this beauty is simply the tree.

Ayn Ulm

A Prayer for My Family

Lord . . .

Keep my family in your loving care.
    Each day in prayer,
    I place them there.

Listen to their souls
    And their humble voices,
    As now they begin
    To face life's choices.

Guide them as they work and play,
    Bless them all,
    Each and every day.

Some so near,
    And others far.
Give each of them, Lord,
    A guiding star.

Patricia Mack

It Is Nice to Sit in Silence

It is nice to sit in silence on a bright and sunny day.
To listen to birds chirping and watch the willows sway.

To contemplate the future and reflect upon the past
To realize what is merely present and treasure what will last.

Time is a precious gemstone, so important for one to bear.
Although we find the quantity, quality time seems rare.

As each day turns to darkness, the present soon is past.
And then before we know it, gone are the shadows the willows cast.

So live each day to the fullest and enjoy the simple things.
Take a moment to appreciate the beauty of a butterfly's wings.

Listen to birds chirping and watch the willows sway.
For it is nice to sit in silence on a bright and sunny day.

Sue Elliott

As a full-time working mother, I find it is easy to get caught up in the distractions of life. This poem is near to my heart because it relays the importance of taking time to appreciate the lasting and meaningful things in our lives. Time goes by in a blink. The special times, the simple times—these are the moments that weave the tapestry of our lives. It is my sincerest desire that these words will inspire others to take time for the simple things.

Let's Pretend

We were only faking it
Just dangling from a thread.
You said you wanted one chance more
Well now, your chance is dead.

We held on tightly to that thread
The thread which made us real.
You were faking through it all
Pretending you could feel.

Tia Wilscam

Deported

He is living in Washington, with a baby on the way
I know he is thinking what will come next?
I am thinking the same, scaring myself
Sharing this thought with my family
Scaring them as well, hoping it doesn't happen
What if's cloud my mind, imagination hitting like lightning
Wanting to avoid reality, even when it's in my face
I can't deal with another person dying
Desperately wishing this stupid war would end
O' Brother please stay strong.

Sydney Walkosak

Lost Pieces

Self-preservation is the first law of nature,
I'm wandering thru the wilderness looking for a savior,
Less of a man than an animalistic being,
Stand up and die rather than kneel down pleading.
The trees cloud my mind and I can no longer see the days go,
Looking past our differences and still . . . no te veo.
My vision seems pointless without seeing my sunshine here,
Thoughts of "us" cloud my mind and now all I can do is tear.
Fear is nothing but a thunder cloud now,
Because it feels strangely familiar not having you around,
Our love was once heavenly but now it's earth-bound.
My heart was once frozen cold,
And in your tears my soul drowned.
All our dreams shattered as the tears hit the ground,
The echoes of past love . . .
I can still hear the sound,
The scattered remains of my broken heart,
Lost to never be found.

Aaron Ocasio

Poetry has always been symbolism for me, a complicated metaphor if you will. A mystery enwrapped in an enigma. This poem is very special to me because it symbolizes the ending of a chapter but a start of a new beginning. This poem is in dedication to my past and future. My hope is to inspire not the world, but one person's world for the better. Hoping to have my words and inspiration be used not for a limited time but a lifetime, I hope to pursue poetry and become a legend and inspiration to people's lives.

Sweet Subzero

The cupcake bushes, frosted white,
Sit in a world of sweet delight.
In the streets, the sugar snow
Crumbles into cookie dough.
The sun shines down as if to bake
Instead of melt this winter cake.
Macaroons up in the sky
Send down aromas, floating by
While children, knowing not how rude,
Run out and, laughing, play with food.

Mary Clare Durel

Puppet

Little puppet boy,
Who pulls your strings?
Who moves your limp little arms,
and your limp little legs?
Who made your mask? It fits you so well.
Who gave you that shallow, painted-on smile?
Little puppet boy,
This dance your learned so precisely with your little wooden brain.
The life you learned to fake with your false wooden heart,
and your blank wooden eyes staring mutely at nothing
as someone moves your mouth,
speaking words that aren't yours.
When will you ever become a real boy?

Shannon Lundstrom

Teardrops

The field is brightened by the moon light,
people see the stars shining,
but I see the moons tear drops sparkling in the sky.
So when I see those tears in the sky I cry too
along with the moon,
but my tears water the grass while those tears
from the moon decorate the night sky.
I don't know why the moon is crying
but I know why I'm crying...
I have a broken heart and I need to let the pain out.
I cry for days and days
so the grass is well watered,
and the sky is well decorated by the moon.
So with my tear drops a beautiful red rose starts to grow
and grow and with every tear it makes the rose grow taller.
and every time the moons tear drops hit the sky a new star is born.
It's amazing how our tear drops make things beautiful,
yet the people crying those tears are in pain.

Stephanie Koehnlechner

The Secrets of Friendship

The secrets of friendship are when you can be so tender with love and compassion like the waves of the ocean almost stern but delicate. I never knew how much people care about each other and somewhere in this world people love. There is a package in every person you meet. There is nothing more better than a package of friendship and with friendship comes interference with the heart and when it comes to heart that means you are the perfect companions for each other and those secrets of friendship keep your life full of friends.

Joann Luna

I Am a Forest

I am a forest,
Pulling my way through life.
Sometimes vines are in my way,
But I always find my way out.
I am a forest as I stand proud.
When people try to knock me down,
My roots are always there holding me up in the ground.
I am like a shelter from the warm, whistling wind,
Watching as all of the animals race around like lightning.
Someday when I hear a bang as I fall down,
I will always remember, I am a forest, proud and strong.

Michelle Zettel

It's Steve, Not Steven

So, what does one write about a man they have never met?
His accomplishments, awards, his roles we'll never forget?

It's hard to say (when there's so much to say.)
But if I would sum it up, I'd sum it up this way:

So few people can portray different people on screen,
But Mr. Carell, well, he makes it look simple, it seems.

You may know him as Evan Baxter, Phil Foster, Michael Scott.
Or perhaps Yorgo Galfanikos (and you thought we forgot...!)

But we know him as Mr. Steve Carell,
A guy who's an actor, and does his job well.

I'm not sure he knows how much laughter and smiles he's caused.
So, let us, as fans, give Steve a round of applause.

Hayley Rueger

A February Night

Like an alley
The street hides between
Trees of brown rattling leaves
In the daring depths of dark.
The swirling wind above

Wrestles itself:
Spinning its airy way
Down the vacant road.

Aged rain water
Leaves its signature in mirror-like puddles
On the impure pavement
And in the mind I call mine.

I fake possession of solitary sight
Enough to spot them
In light's absence.

I playfully splash one:
Shattering its glassy stillness
To beg Childhood's charming return to me.

Amy Cavanaugh

Seasons Pass

You tell me that you need me then you turn around and tell another
that you love her. You lie. Oh you lie lie lie.

You begged and you pleaded even got on one knee. I turned around and
walked away and you never got to explain.
Seasons went by lonely and cold for I stayed the same, lost in a love that
grew to hate because you played the game.

You told me that you love me then turned around and told another
that you loved her. You lie. Oh you lie lie lie.

Oh baby can't you see we could have really been something.
Our love was like wildfire that spread in the heat of summer but then
she happened and then my love grew cold like your soul that perished
during winter.

Oh baby can't you see we could have been really something if your love
wasn't like the season where it comes and goes.

Bridgette Ballard

Stars

The glistening stars of the night,
Are the King's watchers of the light.
Twinkling, so they may seem,
Are really dancers in the heavenly beam.
Dancing on the stage above,
As our Father watches on with utmost love.
They dance fluently, majestically, in full exaltation,
Unto the King, Creator of all creation.
They shine and sparkle as ardent jewels,
Intricate craftsmanship untouched by tools.
He has given His star-light jewels each a name,
A special place, position for each one to remain.
He takes utmost pride and care in His shining dancers of the night,
That He's given us front row seats to see the magnificent sight!

Amy Eismann

My heavenly Father has called me aside. In His presence I am to abide. He has blessed me with the gift, talent, and ability to reveal His truth in the form of poetry. I am to write and tell of His great love, and to save His children from hell. It is with utmost honor and respect upon His word to think, to reflect. That we are but a moment in time, our time is to be used wisely, only to sublime!

This Masquerade

The mask is on,

I hide my shame;
But who's to blame
If not myself,
Here, in this audience of one?

Start the music,

The soundtrack of my affliction begins to play;
Notes of darkness that drive out the day,
Like a black wind.

The ball begins,

And so I dance with my regrets;
No structure, no form, just an eerie silhouette.
But it's all I know,
It's all I've ever known.

The mask is off...

This is me,
And I'm afraid,
To live this life, this masquerade.

Vincent Cuccolo

Fire in Her Eyes

Fire in her eyes
She doesn't wait till the world abides
Like a siren's song she cries
On the ocean that she rides
She dances and it's there she flies
Piercing through these ocean tides
She doesn't wait for the world to see
Like Aphrodite, she'll simply be
With the currents and storms, she remains free
Her sunset colors and gypsy chi
She's like an angel without wings
But she still soars and she still sings
With crimson stars her spirit clings
She wanders till the day she dies
So beautiful the heavens sigh
As she walks above those earthly lies
And there she'll roam,
Forever known
With fire in her eyes

Shaylen Snarski

Friend

A friend is like a flower,
a rose to be exact.
Or maybe a brand new gate that never comes unlatched.
A friend is like an owl,
both beautiful and wise.
A friend is like a ghost, whose spirit never dies.
A friend is like a heart that goes strong until the end.
A friend is like a sister and family.
A friend is like the one who makes you happy,
the one who makes you smile.
Try hard to make it last, because life is so short.

Roseline Achille

Heart

If you're in my heart
Nothing will ever tear us apart
When life is sweet
Our two ends just might meet

Mikayla Hieb

It has always been easy for me to write stories, but it has been even easier to write meaningful poems. Everybody and everything I love inspired me to write this poem. It is an absolute honor to have my poem recognized by you.

You Can Tell

You can tell if someone loves you
   by the beating of their heart

You can tell if someone admires you
   by the glimmer in their eye

You can tell if someone trusts you
   by the firmness of their grip

You can tell if someone depends on you
   by the words they say

You can tell if someone respects you
   by the kisses that you taste

You can tell if someone cares for you
   by the flowers they bring

Love comes in many shapes and sizes
   but it may never die
Like a blazing flame
   deep within your heart.

Alana Bossie

Colors

Paint my world in rainbow
That I hide behind
Cover up the darkness
That lives inside my mind
I'm not showing the world
Who I am inside
I'm stuck here all alone
No one to confide

Paint my world in rainbow
Cover up the lies
When I say I'm happy
But I'm dead inside
Never showing my wounds
Satisfying my pride
Pretending this is me
Like there's no other side

Stephanie Guijarro

Learning from the Pain

I have been hurt in the past by loved ones, family and friends. When you are hurt and broken down so bad you want to get revenge but you know the best revenge is to learn from the pain. I hold my head up high now since I have learned from the pain. I was hurt in all forms but yet I smile now because that pain has taught me how not to treat others. That pain has showed me how low a person can be put down before they get torn apart. I have stopped the pain from within and gave myself a new strength—forgiveness. I have learned to forgive but not to forget so it won't happen again. That pain that once controlled my life has no power now. I am in control of my life and I have chosen that I will not let pain take over again but the valuable lesson is that you can learn from pain.

Carmen Gill-Williams

Motionless

It is as solemn as your footsteps
And as graceful as your smile
That tears your memory
In my mind   secluded   from everything else
I watched your life burn twice.
You

Kathryn Kuszynski

Whirlpool

Anywhere but here
Is where I need to be
There's nothing that can pull me out of this whirlpool
I need an escape

Anywhere but here, anything but this
I can't see up
I can't see down
I'm drowning

Just take me away
Out of this whirlpool
There's no way out
I try to fight it
But that only pushes me farther down
Let me out, I need to breathe

Anywhere but here, anything but this
I can't see up
I can't see down
I'm drowning

Izzy Allen

53359

You were my dream.
I've never been so in love.
Passion burns through my veins.
I die every moment we're apart.
It's you.
Only you.
Take my heart, take my soul, let love be in control.
You are the one, my love.
We withered away in reality.
We don't have it together, but I'm right here.
Forever.

Rochelle Deleon

Word War 3

Our
world in swirls and twirls that twist and circle
with
words of secret and tales that whispers in echo
of
war of screams and takes that wisp-away
our cycle

Whiteeagle Arai

The Horrors of War

Dark have been my dreams of late,
my mind too weary to open this gate.
Horrors unimaginable swirl dark and vast,
and fill my life with fiery blasts.
Gun shots scream into the night
as we fight for all that's just and right.
My friends and comrades in pools of blood soak,
 as they leave this world with the fire and smoke.
Am I next? Is my time drawing near?
In the heat of battle my pride shifts to fear.
People wage war not for pride or fame.
They do it for fun—every war is the same.
The sun arises on the final day.
The war is over. Our job is done. Sanity is all we pay.
But in my mind it plays over and over.
My entire life a simple "No Leaf Clover."
These horrors in my mind will never be done.
Call me a sinner, call me a saint, my only friend a gun.
Dark have been my dreams of late,
my mind too weary to open this gate.

Mikey Campbell

Invisible Words

Maybe if I look at the word long enough I can become that word with no such feeling, besides what the writer gives it.

Let me hide under the deep covers of ink, my whole body becoming the black ink you printed me. I have no mouth, no eyes to seek or see—just another aimless word with someone's eyes looking down on me.

I wish I was a word. Any word would do as long as it'll take away the life I have lived so close to you.

If I were a word I could no longer be in any way a disappointment or feel betrayed.

If I were a word by another persons voice I'd be read.

I'll stare at these words until I myself become a word too.

In any book, short story or poem that'll claim me....

But like life I'll be clustered by other words having no room for my naked arms to spread,

but that's why I want to be a word...any word.

Because I wouldn't have or need arms to spread,

so now I'll sit here yet another day drawing invisible arms on these words, until I myself am a word.

Spreading my invisible arms someone has drawn for me, my naked arms now wide and tattooed with what seems like a never ending hurt and troubles—that like to hide under the crust of my happiness... always there.

That is why I am the invisible word, being unread in silence, hidden in the old pages of an unknown book.

Alyssa Yanez

Poetry is an art, another way I can feel free and myself. "Invisible Words" was written from my fascination for words. So much I long to be a word. Though I realized it can be similar to life in ways we use, read, and spell many words but don't really bother to truly look at them and give them life. That's what I tried to do. Writing is a big part of me. Now I'm learning to share my gift. One day I hope to have all my poetry in a book, starting with this one, which I wrote one day in English class. What else to do with free time?

The Strong Songbird

Be loud.
Don't be afraid to let yourself shine,
show them all that being loud is being proud.
Take leaps and bounds and never slow down,
let the world be your stage and let the world know
your page in the book of life.
And everyone will know 'that girl',
the one who shone like the stars above,
filling the earth with hope and love
through the words that she sang,
through the notes that she rang,
through the memories that she made,
and for the people her voice saved.
Stay proud.
Stay loud.

Ashley Rose

My inspiration behind this poem was the women who always remained strong in their singing, especially the ones who first made the way and who were not ashamed or afraid of how others would see them because of their voice, because they were loud or different or strong. Music, singing and writing have always been special to me. I've always loved to write and sing so it was nice to write something that I could relate both to. I will continue to write and sing in my life and I will continue to be inspired by the women before me.

With a Flame

Everything is worth it
Do what you must
To make the world yours
Have no regrets
And no exclusions
Your life is a party
And you are the host
Do with it what you want
Make it fun
Not only for yourself
But for everyone included
You make the difference
So always try to
Whether things work out
Or they don't
It doesn't really matter
Every step along the way
Has made you who you are today

Kim Anderson

Your Guitar

The placement
of your fingers upon my neck,
  and your core pressed
against my body
    makes me sing.
Without you,
I am an empty tune.

No one
  could have loved me more
cause you,
  my rock star,
    took me home
from that music store.
    Amongst the walls
    of instruments
is where I lay.
  You picked me up,
held me once,
  and instantly knew that I
    was to be yours.

We got home
  you plugged me in,
  turned me on
  and began to play.
Our first song soon flowed
  from the melody
    we made.

    Your voice
    is my matching harmony.
  When you sing along
with the chords you play
    we come together as one,
as if marriage bound
    by our musical romance.

Sasha Heikkila

Does This Make You Proud

I've always been a dreamer
the kind who dreams both night and day
but when I tell them to you, you push them all away
I've dreamed of being an actress
being on stage or on tv
I've dreamed of being a poet
with my poems for all to see
but you tell me to be realistic
how could they possibly come true
but why can't you just see that this is what I want to do
you talk about how proud you are of her and what she's done
you want the same life for me as the one she has begun
but that's not what I want to do
and that's not who I am
you don't believe my dreams will come true
but I'll show you that they can
some of my dreams have come and gone
but there's one that will stay the same
it's the day you'll finally be proud of me
and what I have became

Trista White

Lost in a Thought

Yo this is killa chan speaking out his third eye floating in a sea of space all the time looking for alien races deep inside a conscious mind suddenly to wake in a pure light God spoke to me and showed me a different side of life I exiled the dark and became a glowing spark of energy so bright now I got cosmic waves flowing through my insights I got lyrics that make you think twice I make your mind split like watching someone fight for their life now hold ya chest 'cause your breathing might get tight after I'm done you won't see right so close your eyes and prepare for a ride.

I'm calling on different entities to set me free make my mind overload with knowledge that's never been told like ancient wisdom so wise and old you really think you're decrypting the right code if you even knew it would make your intellect split into atoms so don't act like a savage and think you're following the human passage 'cause you're hopping around life like a lost rabbit don't look at me 'cause you can't handle it just look up in the sky and ask for it.

Yaaaa, my neurological nerves are hypothetically disturbed I'm just sitting down writing down what I heard your mind can't conceive reality 'cause we're all in a blur that's why positive and negative vibes go through your body like a wild herd but still nobody's concerned about the thought patterns that forever burn deep inside your soul like uncovering mysteries that never been told you can't understand this world till you get old so stop trying to fight and realize that life goes on even on a dark narrow road so forget about the cold and never act like you never been told.

It's like going through tombs in pitch black rooms you don't even know what's coming real soon you need to look up in the sky and get in the right tune cause you're too materialistic looking at fancy shoes if you even knew you'd be trying to meditate with the right crew 'cause when the light comes hopefully you're not doomed reincarnation is just a passage to the next casket if your mind doesn't manage it you'll keep returning like savages until your mind expands on it.

I meditate day to day to keep my mind from going insane subliminal messages come at you like a meteoroid from space looking down upon the human race why when we're supposed to upgrade to intellectual race the world is filled with EMP pulses.

Chandler Doyle

I have struggled to overcome two kidney transplants and am trying to find my way through this broken path called life. This poem is a true vision within my deepest consiousness. God bless all for all is God. I meditate day to day to keep my mind from going insane. Subliminal messages come at you like a meteoroid from space looking down upon the human race. Why when we're supposed to upgrade to an intellectual race. The world is filled with EMP pulses—that's why you think your mind is filled with losses but we keep looking up toward the wrong bosses.

The Lonely Highway

The wind blows rampantly on this lonely highway
Specks of dust sting my bare, pale face
Cars pass rarely, but sometimes suddenly

I direct my attention to the faded dashes on this lonely highway
The night is cold, dark, threatening
The crescent moon appears from behind the clouds

It is only I who rides down this lonely highway
Coyotes howl in the distance
The emptiness here is peaceful, but eerie

The lonely highway is still.

Olivia Williams

I Am Mississippi

I am the shrimp boat on the coast,
trying to make a living by catching the most.
I am a musty old oak tree,
Patiently still as decades pass by me.
I am a guitar held by a bluesman,
producing sounds with his withered hand.
I am the mighty hurricane, my winds a' blowing,
I am a twisting tornado, my gusts a' throwing.
I am the majestic white tail dear,
hunted year after year.
I am the sun rising on o'er the Bayou,
shining the light for the morning dew.
I am the tombstone of an ol' Civil War vet,
or the gambler who lost a high end bet.
I am the South in all of its glory,
I am the Mississippi and you know my story.

Dustin Heitzmann

In ninth grade Mississippi studies class, we were asked to summarize Mississippi in a poem. Some wrote of silly and stereotypical things you might often hear, but I chose to think and write about the things that make our state unique and beautiful. Maybe the lovely Gulf as the sun sets and causes the water to jive and glitter, or the stars that shine so bright in the dark Mississippi sky. But I solely believe the content of a poem should come from the heart and your experiences. Even if you write your words down in the period of five minutes, they will echo on forever. And that is why poetry will never burn out or fade away.

Someday

You struggle, toil, and sweat
You push yourself and take the shots
that come your way,
You jump the many hurdles,
and keep moving forward
Waiting for someday
You pass the tests,
Make the cut,
Pull yourself out of a rut,
Waiting for someday
You practice, practice, practice,
You work day and night,
You dream giant dreams,
Waiting for someday,
You hope, pray, and wish,
You make big plans and wonder...
"Someday?"
You gaze up at a clear blue sky
and the sun shines brightly upon your face,
and you whisper to yourself with a smile,
"Someday, someday."

Christine Vincent

I Slept the Sleep of Angels

I slept the sleep of angels
As I lay there in your arms
As if you cast a spell on me
With the magic of your charms
Your loving arms around me
Holding me real tight
As if there to protect me
From the dark shadows of the night
With every kiss you gave me
Seemed to touch my very soul
I only knew then my love
That only you could make me whole
So kiss me now and hold me tight
Love me throughout the night
And in the morning
When we both awake,
I beg dear Lord, not the spell to break

Carol Dornetto

Something Good

True wisdom comes within,
And who is we that makes amends,
Who are we to tell a friend?
Who are we to try to pretend?
Who are we that makes us win?
Who are they that say we can't?
Who are you that points the finger,
or who are they that makes you wonder?
It's you in who that makes the thunder,
That makes the people power stronger,
That makes the hour linger longer,
And when you run from them—
you run from yourself.
So when something good comes to you,
You chase!
Forsake
You say!
Hey—something good is coming my way.

Kimberly Williams

My name is Kimberly Williams and I love poetry. I love to write; something good stems from being able to follow your dreams in life. No matter the negative obstacles that get in your way, you have the inner strength and the power to overcome and challenge the impossible with the power of faith and believing you can achieve success. I come from a large family line and attended San Bernardino High School. I later moved to San Diego, CA, where I still reside as a writer. I wrote my first book Keep'n It Poetically Lyrikal *based on life experiences and my trials and tribulations coming from out of the hard knox of life. I found a new way in life by expressing my inner-man through poetry. I breathe poetry because it is the reflection of love I express to people. My gift of making others feel good is "Something Good."*

If I Could Find the Right Words to Say . . .

I would tell you how I wished I would've been a better mother
I would tell you how blessed I am to have you as a daughter
I would tell you what a wonderful mother you are to my grandchildren
I would tell you how beautiful and kind you are
I would tell you that only God can fulfill every need and desire
I would tell you how much I miss you when I haven't seen you in a
while
I would tell you how incomplete my life would be without you
I would tell you I would have no other as a daughter
I would tell you how very much I love you
If I could only find the right words to say

Mary Ann Cruz

I awoke at 3:30 am because there were words going on in my head. I quickly got up and jotted the words down. That same morning the same words came to me as we were driving to our destination. In my spirit I felt God say this poem is to be given to your two daughters. I wanted to make this gift special so I took a photograph of myself and put the poem in it. I gave it to them on Mother's Day. This was nine years ago. Since then I have lost two sons and only my two daughters remain. My inspiration was God. Will He ever give me other poems? I sure hope so.

#1 Fan

A #1 fan will have posters of you all over their room.

A #1 fan will watch your show every day.

A #1 fan will sing and dance to your music 24/7.

A #1 fan will know ALL the facts about you.

A #1 fan will talk about you day and night.

A #1 fan will have you as their wallpaper in their phone.

A #1 fan will scream "Carlos, I love you!" every second at your concert and have people look at you like you were some kind of psychopath.

A #1 fan will buy BOP magazine every month just to get posters of you.

A #1 fan will get personalized invitations for their birthday party with a picture of you on it.

A #1 fan will have tons of pictures of you saved on their laptop.

A #1 fan will have you as their wallpaper on their laptop.

A #1 fan will have their school binder filled with pictures of you.

A #1 fan will eat your favorite cereal, Fruity Pebbles.

A #1 fan will watch your music video "Worldwide," and press replay 10000 times.

Every day, that #1 fan prays to meet you someday.

That #1 fan is me! Yes, I have done or do all these things.

That's why I consider myself your #1 fan!

Chelsea Rojas

Tomorrow

There is always tomorrow.
Before you know it today will be over.
Once today is over, tomorrow is the next.
If you made it through today,
I guarantee you that you will make it through tomorrow.
If you made it to the next day,
that means you'll be pulling less weight.
The less weight you're pulling,
the further you'll go in the days to come.

Jerry Gawlik

Most of my poetry is based on a life with epilepsy and learning how to deal with it when no medicines or surgery were able to help. In other words, I use my poetry as an emotional and psychological life medicine, but mostly as my life's teacher.

Only Heaven Can Surpass Love

Kissed by an angel,
Some would say
Or cursed by a demon;
Either way

I've come to love,
Yet again I have lost
My heart's all choked up
In turn, death is the cost

But, I remember every minute that I had spent with you,
And I admit that I have to say,
That the word perfect was incapable
Of describing those days

Now I've come to believe that I've been blessed
Even though we didn't last,
Because now I know that there is a love
That only Heaven can surpass

Sarah Goddard

I have always expressed myself through the art of writing. All of my inspration comes from my own life. This particular poem that I have written is about losing someone you love. Even though that love is lost, you still wouldn't take back any of it because being in love is an amazing and rare thing. In truth, only Heaven can surpass it.

The Shadow

Your eyes are so beautiful, when I can see their color.
I love to run my fingers up and down your arms
Until I find the bruises. It breaks my heart.
I wish somewhere behind those dilated pupils,
you could see what I see: a beautiful, amazing person
who is veering with their eyes closed down a path of destruction,
down a path of loneliness and guilt, down a path of regret.
But I know that all you can see right now is the Shadow.
My hand is searching for yours and I am screaming for you to open
your eyes. Come with me in the other direction,
down a path of happiness and bliss . . . Down a path of love.
Just please don't take the hand of the shadow.
It will make you think it can fill your veins with happiness
when in fact, it will make them collapse with hatred.
It will make you think that it is the only one who cares about you
when in fact, it is all of us who are watching you fall into it.
It will make you believe that you can do no better than it,
but give me the opportunity, and I will prove to you that you can.
I know it will be hard but I won't leave your side.
I'll hold your hand through the shakes and the shivers,
I will hold you close through the aches and the pains,
and when you tell me that you "need it,"
I will remind you why you don't.
Your will is strong and so is mine,
and together we can turn your back on the Shadow.

Kristen Parko

This poem was written in honor of someone whom I cared about very deeply. They were enticed, manipulated, and driven under by one of the worst drugs on the market: meth. Meth is used by over 200,000 people nationwide. Not only does it cast a shadow upon its users, but it also casts a shadow upon their loved ones. My heart goes out to all of you who have been affected by the shadow.

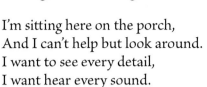

Things of the Night

I'm sitting here on the porch,
And I can't help but look around.
I want to see every detail,
I want hear every sound.

Stars are just appearing,
Fluffy clouds are rolling by.
The sun has now disappeared,
From the darkening sky.

A car passes by,
As the half-moon brightly shines.
The bird feeders have no birds on them,
And the nocturnal animals are coming out to dine.

The lighting bugs are blinking,
The pine trees are standing tall.
A cat sits beside me,
The whippoorwill makes its call.

Toads are croaking happily,
As a cat lazily purrs.
The dogs have stopped their play to rest,
And I can now hear the night peepers.

It's hard to believe,
That God made all these things.
If He can make all this,
Then he is really "King of kings."

Rose Kinniburgh

My name is Rose and I am twelve years old. I was born on July 4, 1999. I am very excited about getting my poem published in this book! I really enjoy writing poetry, and I wrote this poem one night when I was sitting on our front porch. I keep a tablet and pencil under my pillow since at night, in my bed, poems start forming in my head and I want to write them down. When I grow up, I want to be a famous poet and a teacher. So I'm just going to keep working towards that dream. I hope that everybody will follow their dreams.

Tribulations

My parents both drank and fought all the time.
My mental attitude they would undermine.
At nineteen my mother drank herself into her grave.
At twenty four my father died, his bed he had made.
At twenty five I married, but not for love.
Six years later divorce came from above.
Prior to that I'd had four ankle operations.
I broke it on a trip and there were complications.
After the divorce my gallbladder went bad.
Another operation, I was extremely sad.
My mental health was declining fast.
I wondered if happiness would ever find me at last.
But no, a tornado took my home.
I began drinking a lot, I felt so all alone.
Hospitalized for a suicide attempt.
I walked like a zombie with a constant limp.
While in the hospital they found a tumor in my lung.
My sad song continued to be sung.
The pain of another surgery took its toll.
I completely lost my heart and soul.
Major clinical depression and paranoid tendencies.
Financial bankruptcy was only one remedy.
After six shock treatments they told me I had a brain tumor.
I had to withstand all the talk and rumors.
High blood pressure and diabetes take their bodily toll.
And financial worries, I can't get out of this hole.
For a while a new project gave me a goal.
A new thing I could put in my heart and soul.
I am fifty-five with nothing to show.
No good stories to be told.
No legacy to leave behind.
No new dreams to make in my mind.
Karma is not my ally and friend.
My dreams don't come true they only end.
I've never had a chance to just be me.
Remarkable, I don't know, we will see.
Please someone come and help me.
I too have dreams as unremarkable as that may be.

Apaula Roth

A Gift

A voice likened to angels,
As clear as crystal bells.
A heart as wide as the heavens,
And no hate within him dwells.

His virtue is his goodness,
To his honor he does cling.
There is eternal warmth and joy,
When he opens his heart to sing.

He brings the world his passion,
There's glamour to be sure.
But when he sings we dream of things,
We've never dreamed before.

He is God's gift and I am glad.
To have been party to his fame.
His name is Adam Lambert
And I thank God that I was on Earth when he came.

Ronnie Egerton

I came to writing late in life, having never given it any thought at all. A casual acquaintance suggested that I might enjoy writing for helium.com, an internet site. I joined on April 1, 2011 and writing has become very important to me. My stories and poems are generally of a humorous or nostalgic nature and have been very well received by the public. I was thrilled to enter this contest. What better way to pay tribute to my very favorite singer? Unfortunately, mere mortal words can't begin to do him justice.

Haunting Memories

There they are the ghosts of my past,
they never let me just be.
For them I'm the flame that gives them life for all eternity.
I see their faces at the corner of my sleepy green eyes.
I hear their voices as the wind blows by.
The seasons may pass, but they never give it a mind,
for in my mind and heart they lie.
I take them everywhere I go, for their inner grip on me still holds.
Though I may seem to walk free in this world we live in,
I am a prisoner to those hunting memories . . . chained to them I must be,
for I can't ecapse what once was.
I'm no longer that person; I am a friend.

Kirsten Fauquet

We Had to Say Goodbye

God saw you into much pain, so he made us say our goodbyes.
Goodbye is such a hard thing to say, but we cried with pride, but the
hurt was still there.
The feeling of sorrow will not disappear today or tomorrow but in time
it will ease so don't worry about us.
We will forever cherish our memories of you.
We love you and will miss you deeply Rickie Stowe.

Jessie Hamon

Rain

of rain and sun and moon and shine,
the rain, the drops and drips are mine.
though not from clouds this wetness me,
but that of sadness, sorrow be.
for I once knew your touch, embrace,
once saw the lines of laughter, face.
now what's left: precipitation,
grief leaves void of all sensation.
My fingers reach, but feeling not,
my thoughts do cling, fretting "forgot."
remember times of joy and you,
then tears, the rain, leave grassy dew.
But tears that fall for death, despair,
dry up, dry up, in time repair.

Emily Erickson

This poem was inspired by the greatest woman I've ever known, my mom. It was written in the final months after she passed away from liver cancer. Poetry helped me through the grieving process, so to have a poem published is a great honor. It will always remind me of the positive, happy woman, after whom I model my life.

Jon Stewart, a Series of Very Deep Haikus

Birth:
Mister Leibowitz
From New York, to New Jersey
Sagittarius

College:
Soccer team member
Nights with the future Weiner
Many future jokes

Life:
Peabodys, Emmys
Daily Show for years
I miss Craig Kilborn

Forever:
Laughter for masses
Millions every year
I've run out of wit

Emma Opsal

The Law Is Order (haiku)

Scared to confront it,
Everybody else will hide;
Choosing the ladder.

Nowhere to go,
Hope is like a dried up well;
Freedom is broken.

Without any doubt,
It is instinct to fight back;
Hold on forever.

Home run and grand slam,
Without ever taking swings;
The ball is long gone.

Below the surface,
Looking for buried treasure;
No shovel to dig.

Tired from the stay,
The truthful experience;
Competition kills.

America's starved,
Greatest country in the world;
What goes around stays?

United Nations,
Separate America;
Unbearable life.

Williams' shape-spheres,
Actions speak louder than words;
Food and liquor stores.

Abraham Mass-low,
The truth must always be told;
Abraham Lincoln.

Thug motivation,
Instincts protect families;
Inherited needs.

Underground Railroad,
Fugitive -slave acts stopped blacks;
Harriet Tubman.

Technology kills,
Unless you are the hunter;
Survive the hunted.

Empty souls can smile,
Never do they show their teeth;
It is hard to eat.

Working for healthcare,
The "private" sector is rich;
My heart has no hate

Experience yields,
Leadership is foe experts;
Special weapons win.

Feel like a newborn,
Excited for the exit;
I'm already dead.

Adam Lawrence

This poem is an expression of how average individuals seek freedom. My way seeking it has always been through writing. "The Law Is Order" is supposed to demonstrate a particular cry for freedom, no one bent on retribution. Writing has always been one way I have been able to escape pressure as it helps me maintain my civility. I want to thank everyone in my life for supporting me in what I do. Special thank you to my mom Brenda for being the star in my heart. Also, I want to thank God for giving me an opportunity.

Alive

An angel is watching over me with the moonlight as dark as the
demons surrounding the world.
My heart has forgotten the soul that I once loved.

Thinking he has forgotten my name, and my true love
He has always existed in my memory.
Knowing the sin is consuming every breath, I gasp!

Letting the monsters turn my soul in to a dark hole,
And yet I am numb of all the pain.
I never thought I would stop loving, but keep hating.

For one thing is sure that I have let the demons take over me
and reject the one true love that kept me alive.

Meliza Hernandez

A Memory in the Past

There was a time
When I really loved you
There was nobody else besides you
You were the one whom I'd rather die for.

I remember ...
The times that we shared
We were walking hand in hand
Making love on the sand.

You know ...
I didn't want to break up
At times I felt like making up
You were driving me mad
There were times when you made me sad.

I try ...
I try to forgive you
I try to forget you
How long will it last
When you become a memory in the past?

Mark Schroettner

Self Conform

When the trends change, tell me—
who will you be after?
Will you still be the one who taught me
to hold onto laughter?
When the world shifts a pace or so
to the right,
are you the one going left
for the fight?
Will you still see
the multi-colored sky?
Will her majestic beauty
still get you high?
Are you going to
outsmart your common sense?
In ways the heavenly rains
cannot cleanse?
Or HAVE you,
in fact,
discovered
yourself?
Has the world's woolen blanket
of conformity
finally become too heavy,
gotten too itchy?
Can you say
it's harming your health?
Can you say
you have conformed—
to yourself?

Holly Junice

Epic Lambert

so what do you want from me
every day same thing
I have the glamour can't you see
dye the hair, leather clothes, and sing

I am epic yes that's true
my fans are what I live for
the only reason is you
they opened that door

I am here for your entertainment
but if I had you
there is no rearrangement
but who

shall understand the rocking life
I am no sleepwalker
I have no strife
but i am a rocker

I am Adam Lambert
from north, south, west, and east
I am on a shirt
I am clearly beast

Kiera Brady

A Summer Wonder Dream

The summer breeze swiftly blows through the sweet air as dreams
come true,
The life I have is like a bursting rainbow of color, definitely not a sad,
sorrow blue.
I dance until my legs and tummy are achey and sore,
I bust my moves until I literally cannot anymore.
When I sleep in the night, a scene creates in my mind,
I see myself dancing in sequins. I know I really shined.
Believing in myself is something that comes easy to me,
My confidence will really sparkle on stage, you'll see.
As I walk through a meadow of flowers in pink,
I look up at the sky and God sends me a smile and a marvelous wink.
The sunbeams shimmer and the sun finally sets,
Tomorrow will be a good day to make myself shine.
Hopefully, it'll be my best performance yet.

Ally Manciet

The Answer Within

Created by illusions
Miracles dissolving into the night
Spell-binding delusions
That poison the minds
Reality and its truth cannot hide
Deception of lies
To all who wish to awaken the minds
Insight will be given to thee

Created by men
Deception of freedom
With invisible chains
That bind the souls from its reality
But chains will not hold
The souls from their destiny
To all who wish to be free
A key will be given to thee

Time and space and the element of surprise
Be aware of the rapture and the here-after
Enlightenment is the key
Between survival and destruction
To all who wish to know
Wisdom and the knowledge
Will be given to thee

We live in uncertain times
The world is turning inside out
People are looking for answers
But the answer is within each and every one of us.

Tamiko Townsend

Your Name

I wrote your name on a piece of paper but it blew away
I wrote your name on my hand but it washed away
I wrote your name in the sand but the waves whisked it away
I wrote your name in my heart and forever it will stay

Mckayla Ingram

Behind the Curtains of Slander

They tied my wrists high to a tree,
face hid so I could not see,
mouth gagged so not to speak,
lashed with words that were not of me.

Bernice Buri

This is a short poem created from a mental image, one mental image with such a great depth. Behind the slanderous talk, a talk of mere lies destroyed unconditional love from those who loved me. A betrayal. A talk condescendingly toned where compassion was not welcome. The slander and the actions took me to another path to walk. A sad path. A path holding only memories of past feelings and joys. A present where I am alone, shunned and thrown from society and a future unknown.

The Copper Butterfly

On March 31st 1995
a wonderful girl came alive
Sweet, beautiful and caring describes her perfectly
who would've ever thought she would leave this early
She lived life to the fullest
my life without her would be the dullest
14 years in the world
were not wasted by this amazing girl
The copper buterfly now in the heavens once in the trees
will forever be in our memories.

Meleana Rodriguez

This poem is very close to my heart because it was about my friend who passed away September 11, 2009. She was like my twin, so I wrote this poem in memory of her and gave it to her mom on her birthday the following year. "The Copper Butterfly" is one of four poems I have written and all of them have something to do with someone very close to me. I wrote and dedicate the poem "The Copper Butterfly" to the Azuero family in memory of Meghan Nicole Azuero, March 31, 1995–September 11, 2004.

As I Lay Drowning

Washing over my head,
I slipped beneath the waves that flooded my lungs.
My clothes dragged me further into the depths,
further into the blue of your eyes.
I couldn't breathe,
did I even want to? Try to?
Every sharp intake felt like a knife down my throat,
constricting around the blade for dear life.
Life, the thought was a joke,
calling forth from my chapped lips a choked laugh.
What does life matter,
as long as I can drown in the India blue of your eyes?
The ink tinted my skin
as it tainted my love.
Life, what a nightmarish prank.
What does life matter,
as long as I have you?

Sicily Porto

An Ocean of Emotion

She used to be standing right over there,
Smiling, down by the majestic seashore,
Until the waves washed her out of the air.
Without her here, life is a dreadful bore.
Even though she's not here, I still get by.
All I want is to be in her arms again.
On the inside, I just wanted to die.
My efforts to not cry all went in vain.
I traveled back home, feeling all alone;
The world felt empty with her not by me.
Despite happiness being overthrown,
I am not entirely a dead sea.
The water will return her to my life,
For us to never again endure strife.

Ryan Jones

This poem was actually the second and final poetry homework assignment in my twelfth grade English class. This is the third of fifteen poems I have written and felt it was my best. I wrote it back in January 2011, after my girlfriend left to go back home after a visit since she lives out of state. That visit was the first time we walked the beach together and it felt fitting to write a poem about it as a gift and an assignment for school. I wish to thank Mr. John Kelly for all he has done for me.

Beautiful Butterfly / Butherflife

Beautiful Butherflive (Beautiful But her feelings live)Beautiful
Butterfly.
As my warm hands cuddled the cocoon
It started to unravel and hatch
But I had to choose between leaving or to resume
And don't get me wrong it's never been in my nature to be rude
But something deep inside my heart told me I secretly found my
match.
So I watched her arrive, from her toes to her nose, from her eyes and
from the great one above on her feet she arouses right by my side.
A queen and a future mother and an unbelieveable human being that
wants to live the rest of her destiny with me, a king, her king.
A romance that has no tragic end, in which we stay together because
we have two beautiful children.
As her wings opened I felt the breeze of the entire ocean.
As she wrapped them around my neck and I had no choice but to start
stroking. It was more than love, it was her love passion that had me
reacting.
If only your imagination could imagine, you would know what type of
love and trust we have already established.
It was so defined that it came to us like a natural habit.
My butterfly and her beautiful eyes stay gazed upon mine, never
looking away and keeping me guessing.
Just another step into the desert and forest of God's beautiful blessings.
To give her what she needs and wants, I Let her get hers before I even
get started and I feed her when she's in need and bleeds for that time of
month. From the gut, she's mine, no if, ands, or buts.
It's about time that I felt love such as this one, but every butterfly has
its wings in which they usually spread them out and flee to live their
dreams without me in between.
So I have to move on with no memories, just a key to the pain and hurt
that I put away deep inside of me.

Butterflies in the tears from my eyes as they come once every lifetime
because crying is for the weak.
But I gave my all, every second, every chance I got during the week.
So as her wings and dust carried away into the dark, I let her breathe
and gave her a head start while I was still running after her on my own
two feet.
She was so far ahead she didn't even attempt to peek, so I let her go for
good. Beautiful butterfly was just too great, just too gorgeous and had
her own life to operate. So her feelings lived but yet they left.
Memories are only memories until you get a chang of heart.
Now it's my time to change and accept what I have left.

Jeremiah Daniel

That Should Be Me, Don't You See?

Justin Bieber,
You give all the girls a fever
Those beautiful brown eyes,
They just make me wanna hop into a wedding gown
He should wear a king's crown.
I wanna grow wings when I hear the things he sings,
Everyone should bow down when he walks around.
I know some girls try and stalk
But I will wait until he chooses me,
And then the whole world can see
What you, Justin Bieber, really mean to me.

Michaela Bryan

My Dad Was a Hero

My dad was a hero
I knew that to be true
And even though he was one man
There was nothing he couldn't do

But since he was a hero
My dad was never there
He was always out saving the world
And the world never shared

So I didn't see much of my dad
And there wasn't much to say
I guess the world needed him more
Until one day I fell astray

I ran into some problems
And I needed help real bad
But what I needed wasn't a hero
I just needed my dad

He never came to my aid that day
He left me all alone
Because my dad's a hero
And he's never coming home

Stephon Seawright

Cody Simpson

Cody, my favorite song of yours is "All Day",
I listen to it hauling hay,
I listen to it all the time,
I listen to it flipping a dime.

You have moved to LA,
If I ever see you I'll say hey,
You wrote your first song when you were seven,
Everytime I see you I'm in Heaven.

Now it's time to say goodbye,
Hopefully I'll meet you eye to eye,
There's many more things about you to say,
But that would take "All Day!"

Aubry Robinson

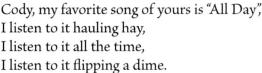

Who Is Bella Thorne?

Bella Thorne,
a girl who is talented in more than one way
she is kind and humble
she supports others and yet is active
although she may be famous she is no different than you and I
Bella is a strong-heartedgirl; she never gives up and that's what makes
her a great person

Ciro Sanchez

*This poem means a lot to me since it's about a person who inspires me to try
hard every day. I hope this poem inspires others to see how great Bella Thorne
really is. She beat dyslexia and made it far in life. Lastly, I would like
to say it's a real honor to have this poem published in this
anthology.*

The Red Picture

I'm alone sometimes,
deleting any other day I have company in my pocket.
I have too much time in my clock,
titling it sideways having minutes fall out the cracks.
My eyes see a little heavier,
slow dancing with Mary's special effect.
Heavier by meaning I see through another pair of eyes.
A new person comes into me,
Schizophrenia at its best and beauty.
Voices in my head that speak out my mouth,
did I just say that or did I think out loud comes to play.
They answer my questions,
as if asking a different person receiving their opinion.
With that, no efforts into losing the breath,
I'd rather spend in need after dancing.
When I'm thinking of the face I see with closed eyes,
I stare at her and wonder what she sees.
My heart had leftover blood so I painted a red picture,
something to look at to pass my time.
Making something beautiful in my mind,
so my attention can be broken.

Anthony Booth

Angel's Writings

Lives are changing
Times has past
Calming of the waters
To make the good times last

Echoes in the hallway
Silence of the dove
Fill the heart with kindness
Turn it into love

Jumping in the meadows
To escape the end of time
Open up the picture
See the different minds

Cry out all the sorrow
Pray for all the times
Charity is for the future
Helping aid the blind

Mark the times past
Look for all the signs
Pen of angels' writings
Here now to cast

Catherine Moore

My Peace

There's in my mind undisturbed by stress,
it's the only place not cluttered by mess.
Whenever I'm pained or scared at all,
let me tell you about the place I withdraw.
It's near a cliff that overlooks the sea,
I go and sit under an old oak tree.
I stay to watch the dolphins play,
and sometimes they speak to say, it'll be okay!
I start to listen to the waves below,
as I sit and watch the sun get low.
I admire the colors the sun gives away,
as it says goodbye to another calm day.
I lay my head down under that old oak tree,
and imagine dreams that are soon to be.
So whenever you're sad or scared a bit,
find me there and we will sit!

Shanna Bracken

Intoxicated with Tattoos

An artist's hand draws steadily near
his canvas alive beneath him
The outline of her dream over her heart
it's perfect-ness she hopes for
His metallic brush dips once
twice into his paint
And the hum of his talent
drowns a heartbeat
Eyes close as her dream comes to life
His living canvas now adorned
the outline of her dream takes form
Again his brush dips into the paint
and her dream comes in vivid color
A bird for her dream to fly on
Its beauty magnificent
Its life now hers
Pride in his work swells her chest
The work has been well worth
the price paid
A thousand times his brushed pierced
his living canvas
Her smile shows she will take her dream
Forever

Holly Sizemore

J.u.s.t.i.n. D.r.e.w. B.i.e.b.e.r.

Just a young kid, singin' his song
Understanding life through a teenage mom.
Someday he dreamed to make it big,
Through youtube, Braun saw something he could dig.
In only a few years a legend was made.
Never Say Never, his dream ceases to fade.

"Don't let anyone stop you" are words he once stated.
Rare yet a beautiful hope he created.
Everything about him is so unique,
When he sings, nothing can ever be bleak.

Because of Justin, it is now known
"I was born to be somebody" and I'm not alone.
Every single fan has hope now
Because of Justin, we go as far as our dreams will allow.
Enthusiasm about God, music and people is his lifestyle
Reminded me to never give up and to always smile.

Casey Anderson

A Treehouse in the Sea

Pointless,
Your words dive into the pores of my forearms
And shiver inside my nerves, like fish scattering
Under a movement of propellers.

Doubtless,
I am that your words lack proper direction,
In a sea which has no land in sight, except
For a wooden monument of your pointlessness
Whose pillars pound through tides,
Dividing that current into seperate upsurges,
Like my thoughts,
Once I attend your matinee
Where you oblige me, your audience,
With you speaking your mind.

Pointless,
Your words float upon my surf
And wade in the pool of my scorn,
Like an irritating squawk of a pelican
Above, who steals my thought processes.

Doubtless,
I am that your robber could get far
In my sea which could consume any boat,
Like a shark craving blood, deep as a fine red wine.

Pointless,
Your words submurge inside of my stomach,
Under my bubbling acids, searching for truth,
Like I had eaten something of yours.
When, in pure truth, you have dove too deep,
And you've been lost for weeks inside of me.

Doubtless,
I am that I ever had any intention,
On letting you leave, escape my restless maze.
You are the mouse whose nose has let you down
And there was no prize in the end, anyway.

Pointless,
Your words pumped adrenaline into your hands,
And your words guided you through my anatomy,
Which was brimmed with ragged coral, hatred you built up inside of
me.
Prying open my jaw, you slipped through, and my anger flooded
Behind you, pulling you back in with my dense, oppressed cyclone.

Doubtless,
I was when you, again, defied me and made your bed
In the middle of my brain.
A treehouse in the sea,
I pushed and rattled your legs which dug into the depths of me,
And I soon found them to be made of steel, made of your ignorance.

I found you pointless.
I found you standing in my path,
And I had no drifts left to wash you away.

Cliff Comfort

*I'm sixteen and it took a while to realize I even liked writing poems. I started
writing short stories and when the end of my sophomore year came around, I
had a chance to be less safe. So, I wrote a poem. After that, I could not stop
writing them. This poem in particular represents a wall, a blockage everyone
may encounter in life. It could be a situation or even a person who stops you
from taking that next stop.*

Index